The Liberated Workplace

Transitioning to Walden Three

William B. Abernathy

Performance Management Publications

ATLANTA, GEORGIA

Performance Management Publications
3344 Peachtree St NE, Suite 1050
Atlanta, GA 30326
www.pmanagementpubs.com

Publisher's Note: This work contains passages that are fictional. Names, places, and characters are a product of the author's imagination. The author has cleverly named the fictional, main character—Sid Murray—in honor of Murray Sidman, a pioneering behavioral scientist. However, any resemblance to actual people, living or dead, or to businesses, companies, events, institutions, or locales is completely coincidental.

Edited by Gail Snyder
Book Layout © 2014 BookDesignTemplates.com
Cover Design—Lisa Smith
1 2 3 4 5 6

The Liberated Workplace: Transitioning to Walden Three
William B. Abernathy
ISBN 978-0-937100-26-4

TABLE OF CONTENTS

Section III: Superior Button's Transition to a Liberated Workplace

This book is about creating a workplace alternative to conventional organizational structures and practices. A conventional organization is defined as one that is managed bureaucratically and pays its employees a wage or salary. The alternative is based on self-managed employees who are paid based on personal and organizational performance.

In 1948, B.F. Skinner published his utopian novel *Walden Two*. Many of the basic concepts and methods described throughout this book are based on Skinner's behavior theory. Skinner was a Harvard psychologist who proposed that psychology had taken a blind alley in choosing to look *inside* the person to understand and manage behavior. Rather, Skinner proposed that the primary causes of behavior were a mutual and continuous interaction between an individual and his environment. This view of human behavior argues that we need not analyze internal motives and personalities to manage people, but should instead analyze and improve their work environment. This book's subtitle, *Transitioning to Walden Three*, is in recognition of Skinner's contributions to the book's development.

The book begins with a discussion of the flaws in the conventional workplace and how these flaws diminish employee earnings, job satisfaction, and job security while severely constraining organizational effectiveness and profitability. This is followed by an overview of theories and principles that underlie the alternative *liberated workplace*.

A case study of Superior Button, a fictional manufacturing company, is presented throughout the remainder of the book in which the owner, Sid Murray, learns about the liberated workplace and then implements such a workplace in his organization. Sid learns how planners, facilitators, and performance-system managers replace traditional managers. Superior Button then proceeds through four transition levels toward a liberated workplace. These levels are I: Results Focus; II: Stakeholder Pay; III: Job Enrichment; and IV: Self-managed Employees. The Superior Button case study is an amalgam of dozens of organizational implementations from which are drawn the management and worker issues, concerns, and benefits of a liberated workplace.

A detailed discussion of Chapter 2 may be found in Abernathy, W.B. (1996), *The Sin of Wages*. A detailed discussion of Chapters 13-17 & 21-22 may be found in Abernathy W.B. (2011), *Pay for Profit: Creating an Organization-wide Performance System*. A detailed discussion of Chapters 18-20 & 22-24 may be found in Abernathy, W.B. (2012), *Human Performance Diagnostics: A Multidisciplinary Approach to Employee Performance Analysis and Improvement*.

Section I:

Conceptual Basis for a Liberated Workplace

CHAPTER ONE

Issues with the
Conventional Workplace

Most organizations rely on the *bureaucratic* organizational structure to manage employees. The bureaucratic structure is made up of a hierarchy of management with one level reporting to the next. Many historians trace this organizational structure back to Sumer (*see http://en.wikipedia.org/wiki/Sumer*) sometime around the year 4,000 B.C. Early on, the bureaucratic model was adopted by the military, which was one of the earliest attempts to get a group of people to act toward a common goal. The purposes of the military management bureaucracy were command and control—to ensure the battle strategy was communicated effectively to large numbers of troops and to provide direct supervision of the troops to make sure they carried out the orders.

Just as the military has generals, captains, sergeants, privates, and so on, the typical organization has a CEO, division managers, department managers, supervisors, and workers. The purposes of the organizational management hierarchy are the same—command and control. Though technology has radically changed since organizations first developed, little has changed in the way organizations are managed. "Once it is fully established, bureaucracy is among those social structures which are the hardest to destroy" (Weber, 1946).

Bureaucratic management is bad for people and bad for organizations. It is bad for people because it relies on aversive control and removes the natural connection between work and consequences. It is bad for organizations because it is expensive, inflexible, unresponsive, and constrains employee performance and commitment.

Bad for People

Bureaucratic management relies on aversive control. The typical wage or salary is guaranteed if an employee shows up for work and performs at a minimal level. Failure to show up or perform at standard may result in warnings, reduced hours, undesirable shifts, poor performance reviews, frozen or reduced pay, no promotions, suspensions, or terminations.

Pay by the day or week is often mistakenly called positive reinforcement; its real function is to establish a standard of living from which the worker can be cut off. (Skinner, 1996)

Aversive Control

This approach to performance management is technically termed *negative reinforcement* in which employee performance removes or prevents an aversive outcome. The reason negative reinforcement is not obvious to management is that employees *avoid* aversive situations by showing up and performing at standard. Consequently, aversive events rarely occur. Negative reinforcement is commonly referred to as *management by exception*. Managers pay little attention to subordinates who show up and perform at standard. However, if either of these requirements is not met, the manager threatens the employee with an undesirable outcome. By-products of a reliance on negative reinforcement include minimal performance, stress, absenteeism, and turnover.

Disconnected Outcomes

Bureaucratic management also severs the natural relationship between work and the benefits of work. This is because pay is not directly related to performance. Instead, pay is determined by the perceptions of the manager. Most entrepreneurs create organizational cultures they would never work in themselves. If they did, they would never survive the close supervision, bureaucratic decision-making, and the demands for a strict adherence to rules and policies. Executives at the top of an organization's pyramid are free to create and innovate, but as you move down the pyramid more and more restrictions regarding what can and cannot be done are enforced. William Whyte's book, *The Organization Man* (1957), remains one of the best descriptions of how repressive corporate life can be.

Bad for Organizations

There have been major advances within organizations with regard to equipment, communications, logistics, and data systems, but no essential change in the way organizations are managed. Though the bureaucratic system has served its purpose, from the beginning it was flawed and today it is becoming impractical. Four inherent flaws in organizational performance created by the bureaucratic system are expense, inflexibility, unresponsiveness, and mediocre employee performance.

Expense

In many organizations employee compensation and benefits may consume as much as 70 percent of operating expenses. Bureaucracies are expensive in that they require a costly management overhead. The more organizational levels and the tighter the management span of control, the more the expense. This expense is further increased by the bureaucratic notion of *job specialization*. Employees are restricted to narrowly defined job roles to reduce the number of functions that a manager trains and supervises. To ensure all functions are performed, the organization must provide redundant employees in these job positions since an employee absence would prevent the performance of the function. The result of multiple layers of management, tight management span of control, and job specialization is excessively high labor costs which reduce an organization's competiveness.

Inflexibility

To prosper in today's business environment, companies require a flexible organization that capitalizes on individual employee creativity and initiative. Only in this way can they respond to the rapid changes that are constantly encountered. In the American culture, we have admired entrepreneurial innovation and risk-taking because these are the people that make our culture successful for all of us. It is time to extend these opportunities beyond the entrepreneur to the workforce. Bureaucracies, with their close supervision and rules, discourage innovation and flexibility. Bureaucratic inflexibility has also restrained organizations from moving to virtual workplaces in which employees work at home via the Internet. These environments simply do not allow for conventional, direct supervision.

Unresponsiveness

In a bureaucracy, the manager is the source of most rewards and punishment. It is the manager who controls job assignments, reviews the employee's performance, and makes decisions regarding pay increases, promotions, and terminations. It is therefore natural for employees to focus inward on their manager rather than outward on customers and competitors. As a result, the organization is less responsive to external changes.

Mediocre performance

Today's employee is often little committed to the organization. She will quickly abandon the organization for a competitor who offers a small gain in compensation or status. Thousands of the best employees leave organizations each year to start up their own companies— often as competitors. Absenteeism and tardiness are common.

Productivity research finds employees, even in the best organizations, are producing at only a fraction of their potential.

Today's organization can no longer afford mediocre performance. Our experiences with clients find that simply introducing objective performance measurement and incentive pay will yield an average and sustainable 33 percent improvement in all types of employee perfor-mances, as the chart below illustrates. This finding tells us that conventional management practices force compensation expense to be a third more than it should be. Much larger increases in employee performance are possible if the organization gradually moves away from conventional management toward the liberated organization to be described in this book.

Does it seem to you unreasonable to estimate that the present efficiency of society is of the order of a fraction of one percent? (p. 293, Skinner, 1948)

1st Year Average Performance Improvement
After Performance System Implementation

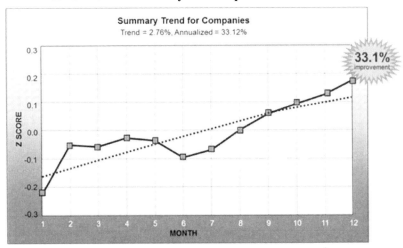

Average Performance Improvement for a Sample of 2,195 Matrix Measures

(Abernathy, 2000)

Management and management theorists have looked for answers to performance issues in all the wrong places. Books are written about the "X" and "Y" Generations. The problem is often seen in the people themselves. They have no will to work. Or, the problem is in the organization's leadership. The number of books published each year on leadership, management, and supervision is nothing short of astonishing. Others argue that employees lack teamwork. Another school of thought blames employee performance issues on poor work processes. Employees want to work but inefficient methods prevent them from doing so.

Some truth exists in all of the above answers. However, these solutions follow the adage of *not seeing the forest for the trees*. The larger issue is the organization's bureaucratic performance system. Organizations have accounting systems, logistics systems, manufacturing systems, and management information systems. These systems are often transportable from one organization to another or can be purchased from vendors.

Each organization also has a performance system. This system consists of the organizational and managerial structures and practices that direct, guide, facilitate, evaluate, and motivate employee performances. Organizational performance systems are usually homegrown. Unlike the other organizational systems, performance systems more often evolve than they are planned. Though managing products and services are complex processes, few people would argue that the processes that impact employee performance are somehow less complex.

We have sophisticated systems for managing products and services while relatively primitive systems for managing people. What has caused this state of affairs? Why are we so good at managing things and so bad at managing people? The first reason is that we *are* people. Managers simply do not react to other people in the same way they do to things and processes. The manager's practices are determined by his past experiences with family, friends, and coworkers. The manager naturally tries to understand and interact with subordinates using techniques that have worked for him in past social situations. Unfortunately, doing so leads to major variations in managerial effectiveness and how employees are treated within an organization.

A second reason people manage performance poorly is our long history of looking for problems and solutions to poor performance within the person rather than in the person's situation. Managers talk about a lack of employee traits like cooperativeness, dedication, commitment, work ethic, and the like, when asked to explain unsatisfactory performance. These explanations are circular reasoning. Why doesn't Mary meet her deadlines? She lacks the work ethic, motivation, or dedication. How do you know this? Because she doesn't meet her deadlines.

A third reason is lazy management. It is easier for the manager to blame the employee, rather than herself, for poor performance. As a college teacher, a common comment I heard in the faculty lounge was, "If I only had good students, I could teach!" It is arguable that if all students were good students we wouldn't need teachers. Why should the manager put forth the effort to analyze the work situation and his management practices when he can simply blame employees for poor performance?

The alternative to bureaucratic management is described in this book. To accurately portray the design and implementation of a liberated workplace, a case study, *Superior Button*, is presented in the second section of the book. Superior Button is an amalgam of the author's consulting experiences with numerous clients. For simplicity, Superior Button is a small factory, but the same issues and methodology apply to any type and size of organization.

References

Abernathy, W.B. (2000). An analysis of the results and structure of twelve organizations' performance matrix and incentive pay systems. In (Eds.) L. Hayes, J. Austin, R. Houmanfar, M. Clayton. *Organizational change.* 240-272. Reno, NV: Context Press.

Skinner, B.F. (1948, 1976, 2005). *Walden Two.* Indianapolis: Hackett Publishing Company.

Weber, M. (1946). Bureaucracy, In *From Max Weber*, eds. Hans Gerth and C. Wright.

Whyte, W.H. (1957). *The Organization Man.* New York: Doubleday & Co.

Chapter 2

The Sin of Wages

Positive vs. Negative Reinforcement

Positive and negative reinforcement are both methods for increasing the frequency of a desired behavior. Positive reinforcement increases desired behavior by giving something of value to the employee where negative reinforcement increases desired behavior by postponing, preventing, or removing aversive situations such as criticism, a bad performance review, probation, or termination. Positive reinforcement employs incentives while negative reinforcement relies on threats.

Both methods can be used to manage behavior. The introduction of wages and salaries has disconnected an employee's performance from his pay. He is paid by the hour rather than for what he has produced. Consequently, managers are forced to use negative reinforcement (threats) to manage employee performance since the positive reinforcer of *pay*, is no longer available as an immediate management tool. Put simply, in the conventional management system an employee doesn't work to earn his pay, he works to avoid losing it.

The baseball manager Casey Stengel put it this way, "I like my players married and in debt. Then I know I can manage them." The notorious mining company stores had miners run up debts they could not pay off to ensure they continued working in the mines. In my earlier book, *The Sin of Wages* (Abernathy, 1996), I described at length the seven *sins* of the conventional wage-and-salary system. Briefly, they are as follows:

1. *Fixed-Cost Pay*—Wages and salaries are guaranteed, fixed costs. When revenue declines, fixed-cost pay does not adjust, placing the organization and its employees at risk. When revenues increase, employees work harder but often receive no additional pay.

Another flaw in the fixed-cost pay system is the practice of annual merit increases in which employees get a percentage increase in their base pay. These increases grow at a compound rate and exacerbate the above problem if they grow faster than the company's price increases or productivity.

2. *Pay for Time*—When companies pay people by the hour, they discourage employee efficiency. Efficiency is simply not in the best interest of the employee because it can result in less overtime, reduced hours, or job loss. Further, pay for time shifts the focus of management from results to time. Management is concerned with overtime, under time, compensatory time, part-time, and full-time rather than results.

I once worked with a bank's Credit Card Application Processing Department. Credit card approvals were requiring 27 days to complete. Overtime was a constant issue. I suggested to the department's management that we allow the employees to go home with a full day's pay when the work was completed. They argued that this would be too expensive. This concern illustrates the problem with focusing on time. We forget about productivity. If the total labor cost for the day is 10 employees X $20.00/hour X 8 hours = $1,600, and the number of applications processed is 200, then the labor cost per application is $1,600 / 200 = $8.00. If the employees finish 200 applications in one hour rather than the normal eight, and still receive a day's pay, the labor cost per application remains the same. Labor cost per unit is the important issue—not hours worked.

After this discussion, the department manager agreed to let the employees go home and receive a full day's pay as soon as they finished the applications for the day. Under this program, the employees were able to go home around noon each day. The delay in credit card approvals was reduced from 27 days to 9 days at no cost to the department. In fact, the reduction in overtime pay, and the additional interest on credit card purchases due to quicker approvals, substantially reduced the net labor cost per application processed.

3. *Corporate Socialism*—The conventional pay system pays all employees in the same job position about the same—regardless of their actual contribution to the organization. Pay is based on the employee's market value rather than her performance. For example, in the above credit-card example, the labor cost per application was $8.00. The 10 employees were processing 200 applications a day or an average 20 applications per each employee.

But, in fact, some employees processed more than average and some less. If employees were paid $160 a day ($20/hour) an employee who processed 30 applications a day only cost the organization $160 / 30 = $5.33 per application while an underperformer who processed only 10 applications cost the organization $160 / 10 = $16.00 per application. This practice is unfair to high performers who often regress to mediocre performance as a result.

4. *Entitlement Thinking*—Wages and salaries are seen as entitlements by employees because they are paid for time rather than results. This disconnect between company profitability and employee pay produces an us-vs.-them employee

view of management and ownership. Employees see profit as always at their expense.

5. *Competition and Cooperation*—High performance is discouraged by other employees since it may lead to more difficult work standards. High performance is often rewarded through promotions to management. This practice discourages cooperation among employees vying for the same management position. We want our employees to compete with other companies—not with each other. Further, this practice removes the best performers from their jobs and may place people in management who lack the requisite skills or interests.

6. *Management by Perception*—The wage-and-salary system requires only a time clock to determine an employee's pay. Consequently, results measures are replaced with easier annual reviews based upon supervisor perceptions of employee performance. These perceptions are, as often as not, based on employee likeability rather than performance. Psychologists refer to our willingness to overlook the shortcomings of a person we like as the *halo effect*. This effect has been well researched and documented. Employees learn that getting along with the supervisor is more important than producing results.

7. *Management by Exception*—Without objective performance data, managers and supervisors are forced to manage by exception (negative reinforcement). That is, they criticize mistakes but rarely comment on good performance. This is because they usually know when something goes wrong but often have no information on what goes right. As a result, employees focus on avoiding errors and blame, which

reduces initiative and productivity. This is a common theme in many bureaucracies. "You have to go along to get along."

References

Abernathy, W.B. (1996). *The Sin of Wages*. Atlanta, GA: Performance Management Press.

Skinner, B.F. (1996). *Upon Further Reflection*. New York: Prentice Hall.

Chapter 3

The Free Operant

B.F. Skinner is known for his theory of behavior and especially for his concepts of positive and negative reinforcement. Most people are less familiar with a key distinction he drew between traditional psychology's response and his concept of the *free operant*. Earlier formulations viewed behavior as a response that was elicited by a stimulus. In contrast, Skinner viewed most human behavior as emitted and then shaped and sustained by environmental consequences. He thought the elicited response was too restrictive and mechanical to adequately explain the variety and complexity of human behavior.

Skinner defined an *operant* as a class of behaviors that produce a common result. A person's preference for specific behaviors is guided by how efficiently they produce the desired results. The operator is free to determine the best solution through exploration and at her own pace. This is a very different perspective from that of industrial engineering where experts determine the ideal behaviors and then require employees to perform within narrow behavioral guidelines. Statisticians, like Edward Deming, see variation in behaviors as a problem. The free-operant view sees variation in behaviors as a necessity for continuous improvement and adaptation. The real issue is variations in results—not behaviors. In Skinner's view, people are not automatons that are pushed around by environmental stimuli. Rather, they actively engage the situations they find themselves in with curiosity, exploration, and learning. Through exploring their environments, they learn the best means for optimizing their effectiveness in various situations.

Skinner's theory of the free-operant parallels, Charles Darwin's natural selection, and economist Adam Smith's free market: The common points in these three concepts are the importance of variation and selection. Genetic variation (mutation) is central to Darwin's theory of evolution. Mutations that make the organism more likely to survive and procreate are selected by the environment (survival of the fittest).

I have called this principle, by which each slight variation, if useful, is preserved, by the term Natural Selection. (Darwin, 1859)

Similarly, the selection of goods and services by customers is the foundation of the economist Adam Smith's free market.

Every individual necessarily labors to render the annual revenue of society as great as he can. He generally neither intends to promote the public interest, nor knows how much he is promoting it . . . He intends only his own gain, and he is, in this, as in many other cases, led by an invisible hand to promote an end which was not part of his intention. (Smith, 1776)

A farmer harvests his crop and sells it to a granary. The granary then pays another organization to transport the crop to a food processor that then sells the product to a distributor. The distributor sells to a grocer, who then finally sells the product to a consumer. Who manages this complex process? The marketplace drives it. In each transaction one party is a seller and the other is a buyer. Their mutual interests coordinate each transaction. There is no leader—only a marketplace or what Skinner termed *contingencies*.

Individual organisms mutate genetic variations that alter behaviors or structures that are, if useful, sustained by their environments. Individuals in a free market try various approaches to making a living and continue those that prove successful. People explore new situations to determine the best means of functioning effectively within them.

These principles have much in common and are termed *selectionist theories*. Unfortunately, they are often poorly understood and misinterpreted.

This misunderstanding stems from our Western interpretation of human behavior in terms of cause and effect. We look for a prior cause that will explain a person's behavior. Surely, a chicken can't look and act like a chicken simply through selection of random variations in the chicken's genetic code. An economy can't operate simply through selection by the marketplace of desired goods and services and their prices. An individual's social and work behaviors can't simply be the result of selection by the situations to which they have been exposed. We intuitively look for a first cause– a creator, economic planner, or character trait to explain why things are as they are.

Karen Pryor describes this confusion with respect to her highly successful application of free operant principles to animal training.

> They (traditional animal trainers) seem to find this absence of an initial "command" even more baffling." How does the animal know what to do?" "He doesn't," we say. "He's finding out for himself." It's fundamental societal behavior, but quite different from dominance and submission. This kind of training involves a two-way communication. It's a bargain, a shared endeavor, and a business agreement. (Pryor, 2000)

Zen Buddhism

A related philosophical view to Skinner's free operant theory or 'radical behaviorism' is Zen Buddhism. Roger Bass (2010) points out that behavior analysis and Zen preserve no subject–object distinction: "When contingencies are the units of analysis, the individual is part of a mutual interactive context. Zen's central notion of the individual-inseparable-from-the-world is consistent with behavior analysis and evolutionary biology."

Similarly, Diller and Lattal (2008) state: "When these rules are observed, it is possible to identify the impermanent and interdependent nature of all things. Here, impermanence is conceptualized as a state of constant change and a lack of static entities. Interdependence is the concept that everything that exists in the universe is linked to every other thing; the actions of a single individual have ramifications for everything else that exists."

The universe is uncaused, like a net of jewels in which each is only the reflection of all the others in a fantastic interrelated harmony without end. (Balsekar, 2000)

The selectionism system view is then, widely held in behavioral science, biology, and economics as well as eastern religion. It is a difficult perspective for Western managers to adopt, but is well worth the effort to a further understanding of how organizations operate.

Rule-Governed vs. Contingency-Shaped Behavior

Bureaucracies operate more on rules than contingencies. Skinner described the differences between what he termed *rule-governed behaviors* and *contingency-shaped behaviors* (Skinner, 1969). By *contingency*, Skinner means an if-then relationship, or "If I do this, that will likely happen."

Rule-Governed Behavior	Contingency-Shaped Behavior
Maintained by sanctions	Maintained by natural consequences
Contrived	Natural
Maintained by culture	Maintained by universal consequences
Constricted	Variety and richness

Rule-governed behavior refers to behaviors that are prescribed by formal rules. For example, posted speed limits are rules. We drive within the speed limit on a lonely road because of the rule—not necessarily natural consequences. Conformity to rules is usually enforced through aversive control or sanctions. We are assessed a fine for exceeding the speed limit, but we are never pulled over and given an award for driving the speed limit.

Contingency-shaped behaviors develop through interactions with consequences. For example, today I play the piano because my behavior is reinforced by the sounds I produce and listener recognition. However, as a child I hated taking piano lessons because my playing was prescribed by the teacher's rules. If I failed to play in the prescribed way, my piano teacher admonished/corrected me, which was punishing. We express our preference for contingencies vs. rules when we say, "Don't tell me what to do. I'd rather do it myself!"

Since rules necessarily dictate behaviors that are not often naturally reinforced, they must be artificially maintained by the organizational culture and managers. In contrast, natural contingencies do not require contrived interventions to remain effective. The natural consequences of a successful business enterprise are profits and customer loyalty— to name a few.

Though all organizations, or for that matter all social interactions, must have general rules within which people operate, innovation and progress come from variations in how people work within these rules. The British philosopher Gilbert Ryle provides the following anecdote to explain this point.

A scientifically trained spectator, who is not acquainted with chess or any other game, is permitted to look at a chessboard in the intervals between the moves . . . After a time he begins to notice certain regularities . . . He commiserates with them (the players) on their bondage. "Every move that you make," he says, "is governed by unbreakable rules; from the moment that one of you puts his hand on the pawn, the move that he will make with it is, in most cases, accurately predictable."

Heartless necessity dictates the play, leaving no room in it for intelligence or purpose/" . . . *The players, of course, laugh and explain to him that though every move is governed, not one of them is ordained by the rules.*

Though nothing happens that is irregular, plenty happens that is surprising, ingenious, or silly . . . *The rules are the same for all the games of chess that have ever been played, yet nearly every game that has ever been played has taken a course for which the player can recall no close parallels. (Ryle, 1949)*

Creating a Free-Operant Organization

It is a sad situation that most contemporary animal training now relies on positive reinforcement while the management of people remains centered in coercion. Why is this? It is because we don't really trust natural consequences as a means of management. We are more comfortable when there is a leader. This is the heart of the debate between those who promote a free-market economy vs. those who demand government planning and intervention. The traditional way of thinking is that we need to tell people what to do— not count on them to figure it out.

Hundreds of books have been written on how to get employees committed to organizational objectives and long-term success. Many of these prescriptions rely on improved communications (telling people what to do—but better). Employees are provided mission statements and annual objectives. We tell them what we want, and then we tell them again. This approach rarely gets the results we hope for, and employee behavior usually drifts back to behaviors that are comfortable and safe. Four key ingredients are needed to create a free-operant workplace.

1. *Personal Consequences*— First and foremost, the desired outcomes may be accurately communicated, but there may be no direct connection between achieving these outcomes and any personal benefits to the individual employee. Again, as Adam Smith put it, *"He generally neither intends to promote the public interest, nor knows how much he is promoting it . . . He intends only his own gain . . ."* The secret then, is to arrange personal consequences for each employee that align with and drive the organization's overall objectives.

2. *Focused Performance Measurement*—Second, the impact of day-to-day behaviors on strategic and financial organizational results is often ambiguous to the employee. The employee may know what to do, but she may not know why she is doing it. The solution is to develop and track performance measures that align with organizational objectives and are directly actionable by employees. These measures provide feedback and reinforcement to employees that are essential for continuous improvement.

3. *Positive Leadership*—The most difficult free-operant transition problem is changing management practices. Manager experiences are with direct supervision, enforcement of organizational rules, management by exception, and subjective performance evaluations. These practices are obstacles to the implementation of a free-operant workplace. Three methods can assist in the transition to positive leadership: management training, upward feedback from employees concerning management practices, and increasing manager span of control. The greater the span of control, the more difficult it is for the manager to persevere in traditional supervision practices.

4. *Stakeholder pay*—To energize employees to pay attention to key results, and to seek out ways to improve these results, the employee must have a stake in both personal and organizational achievements. This means the employee shares the business risks and rewards with the organization by accepting a less guaranteed wage or salary in exchange for an opportunity to significantly share in organizational profits. If you want employees to think and act like partners, they must be paid like partners.

Stakeholder pay is then, similar to self-employment. The organization is the employee's customer and the employee the supplier. The advantages to the organization are consistent alignment of employee performances with strategy and much less need for direct employee supervision. The advantages to the employee are a reduction in aversive control, more empowerment, and a greater personal earnings opportunity.

Organizational Benefits of a Free-Operant Workplace

Adopting the free-operant or liberated view of management yields many benefits to the organization and its employees. Four benefits are particularly valuable—strategic alignment, organizational adaptability, employee commitment, and optimal performance.

Strategic Alignment

In a liberated organization, managers determine tactics based on organizational strategy, organize workflow across departments, and provide employees the resources, knowledge, and skills needed to perform successfully. However, managers no longer directly supervise employees. Employees are managed by the natural consequences of good or poor results as defined by performance measures that align with organizational strategy and profitability. In a stakeholder pay system, good performance provides above-market pay while poor performance results in below-market pay.

Organizational Adaptability

Organizational change is usually difficult and slow. Fifty years ago the pace of change for organizations was manageable. Today however, globalization and rapid changes in technology and the marketplace require successful organizations to be much more nimble and responsive to change than ever before. This capability will not occur if we continue to manage the organization in the same way we did 6,000 years ago. It is now essential that employees focus on the marketplace and profitability each and every day. They must respond quickly and effectively to changes to ensure the success of the organization. A flexible, responsive, and innovative employee group requires a radical change in organizational management practices. We need to move away from direct supervision, aversive control, and entitlement pay toward paying directly for measured results that drive organizational success.

Employee Commitment

Employee commitment is defined operationally as staying with the organization, consistently performing well, and helping outside the assigned job area. Stakeholder pay has been shown to significantly reduce turnover, increase employee interest in improved profitability, and to optimize employee performance. Converting management from subjective, aversive control to objective, positive reinforcement encourages free-operant behaviors such as innovation, initiative, self-management, and expanded work repertoires.

To optimize and sustain employee performances, management practices must change from traditional supervision to facilitation. The new manager must be knowledgeable and skillful in analyzing performance problems and implementing solutions. The new manager must ensure each stakeholder employee has the opportunity to perform, the capability and resources to do their job, and a supportive job context that minimizes aversive events and maximizes performance feedback and positive reinforcement.

The liberated workplace is a practical, alternative management system to the traditional bureaucratic hierarchy. The system requires objective performance measurement, stakeholder pay, and a change in management practices. The results of system implementation are dramatic and sustainable improvement. Imagine an organization with 1,000 employees. In the conventional system, the people concerned with the organization's profitability and sustainability may number no more that 20 or 30. In a free-operant workplace, this number increases to up to 1,000 with all employees concerned about the success of the organization.

References

Balsekar, R. (2000). Advaita, the Buddha and the Unbroken Whole. Zen Publications.

Bass, R. (2010). Zen and behavior analysis. *The Behavior Analyst*, 10: 83-96.

Darwin, C. (1859). *On the Origin of Species by Means of Natural Selection, or the Preservation of Favoured Races in the Struggle for Life*. London: John Murray.

Diller, J.W. & Lattal, K. (2008). Radical behaviorism and Buddhism: complementarities and conflicts. *The Behavior Analyst*, 31: 163-177.

Pryor, K. (2000). Latham Letter.

Ryle, G. (1949). *The Concept of Mind*. London: Hutchinson.

Skinner, B.F. (1969). *Contingencies of Reinforcement: A Theoretical Analysis*. New York: Meredith Corporation.

Smith, A. (1977) [1776]. *An Inquiry into the Nature and Causes of the Wealth of Nations*. University Of Chicago Press.

Chapter 4

Behavior Systems Theory

A *behavior system* is a complex array of interacting behaviors and environmental contingencies. Examples of environmental contingencies external to the organization (metacontingencies) are those generated by investors, suppliers, customers, competitors, technology, governmental agencies, and the economy. Examples of contingencies internal to the organization (performance system) include employee selection methods, training, compensation, promotions, pay, management practices, organizational structure, and work processes.

All organizations are behavior systems. Some systems are highly organized while others are rather chaotic. Some systems advance the objectives of the organization while others impede ownership and management from achieving their goals. Some systems foster employee commitment and high performance while others promote high turnover and mediocre employee performance. Some behavior systems create a flexible and responsive organization while others produce a rigid, apathetic employee group.

Many examples of systems exist. If you replace your car's fuel injection, but the transmission is not working, the car will not run. If you have a heart transplant but your kidneys fail, you will still be in poor health. An organization is also a system. A systems view argues that strategies that address parts of a system, without standing back and observing the interrelationships of the whole system, will likely produce short-term improvements that are unsustainable. Further, such a molecular approach could produce unintended effects (the butterfly effect) in other aspects of the system that ultimately reduce the total system's effectiveness.

Piecemeal approaches to the installation of a performance system will likely harm interdependencies across jobs. A focus on an outcome in a particular job position may constrain performance in other job positions. For example, a focus on reducing errors in sending job positions may result in delayed input in receiving jobs. Further, measuring and reinforcing one job dimension (for example, sales commissions) may signal to employees that other dimensions such as margins, on-time payment, and inventory are unimportant. The result may be a reduction in performance on these unmeasured dimensions.

The biggest problem with piecemeal strategies, however, is that they are unsustainable. When a piecemeal implementation is made, the larger system fails to support the change. This happens because no true systemic changes were made. The organizational environment within which managers and workers operate remained unchanged. Without a change in the system, entropy will naturally take place.

Complexity Theory

The Gestalt psychologists of the 1930s stressed that the organizational whole was greater than its parts. They objected to piecemeal approaches to psychology. Ellis wrote the following:

The fundamental "formula" of Gestalt theory might be expressed in this way. There are wholes, the behaviour of which is not determined by that of their individual elements, but where the part-processes are themselves determined by the intrinsic nature of the whole. It is the hope of Gestalt theory to determine the nature of such wholes. (Ellis, 1938)

More recently, *complexity* theorists have argued this point from the vantage point of systems and information theory.

Complex, adaptive, dynamic systems exhibit system-level structure and behavior that cannot be fully specified from a detailed understanding of isolated system components. (Arrow, et. al., 2000)

A key premise of behavior systems theory is that organizations cannot be well understood, nor significantly improved, by a direct examination or manipulation of the behaviors of particular members of the group. Organizations are complex systems. To fully understand and reengineer the myriad functional relationships within an organization, key outcomes that describe the purpose of the entire organization must be the ultimate rationale for analyzing and determining system changes.

As the number of parameters required for the complete description of a system increases, so does the complexity . . . By changing the question at hand or the functional relationships, one can reduce the degree of complexity. Instead of inquiring into the molecular events of mutation, for example, one might ask only whether the mutants survive. (F. Cramer, 1993)

The survival of a business organization is determined by profit. The objective of the system begins with profit and is judged by its impact on profit. A behavior systems technology helps the organization survive by ensuring profitability.

Self-Regulating Systems

I have described how selectionism emphasizes the role of the environment in human behavior and reverses our common way of looking at cause and effect. A final concept from systems theory is important for a full understanding of behavior system theory. This is the concept of self-regulating systems. A self-regulating system is one that senses changes in the environment and automatically adjusts its functions to those changes. A thermostat is a simple example of a self-regulating system. If the temperature drops, the thermometer senses this and activates the furnace. When the temperature arrives at the desired setting, the thermostat deactivates the furnace. Self-regulating systems depend upon timely and precise feedback from the environment to operate successfully.

Most of us, however, are suspicious of self-regulating systems and find them mysterious or even threatening. Movies like *Dr. Strangelove*; *2001: A Space Odyssey*; and *The Terminator* illustrate this fear. Machines or natural systems that seem to run themselves trouble us. In earlier times, Animism attributed a soul or spirit to inanimate systems that appeared to function independent of human intervention.

Central planners have a similar suspicion of self-regulating economic systems. They cannot accept that the marketplace can self-regulate effectively. Instead, they want a central plan and leaders that regulate economic activity. A planned economy was tried on a grand scale in the Soviet Union. The results were not good. In the United States, smaller-scale, central economic intervention, such as price controls have fared no better. Self-regulating systems are often very complex and beyond the understanding of the would-be interloper.

This suspicion of self-regulation is often also the case with organizational leadership. Organizations are similarly complex and often the subtle and dynamic interactions within the organization, and between the organization and its environment, are not well understood by those in charge. In an open-network behavior system, ownership and management establish the general rules of the game through an analysis of the organization's metasystem. These rules define the desired business and social outcomes of the organization. The rules are then translated to objective performance measures that enable the employees to self-regulate their performances.

Metasystem

An organization is made up and governed by many overlapping systems. Three levels are the metasystem, support system, and the performance system. These systems interact within and across levels. The metasystem is made up of systems outside the organization that influence it and include technology, government, the marketplace, and the social system. In the open-network behavior system, the executive leaders (planners) research and develop strategies to respond to changes in the organization's metasystem. These changes are communicated to individual employees and employee teams through revisions to the employee performance measures, goals, and priority weightings.

Support System

Examples of support systems within the organization include logistics, data management, accounting, and marketing which influence the effectiveness of the organization. The organization must ensure these systems are functional to optimize the performance of the employee teams and the overall organization.

Performance System

A third sub-system consists of those organizational processes that have a direct effect on employee behavior. These include human resources, organizational structure, policies, job definitions, work processes, workflow, work management, work group, customers, and supervision. *How this subsystem can be reengineered to optimize employee behavior is the focus of this book.*

Bureaucratic vs. Open-Network Systems

Larger organizations have relied on the bureaucratic management structure for command and control of its members. An alternative organizational structure is the *open network*, in which various jobs and departments interact directly with little vertical direction. This approach significantly reduces management overhead, and increases responsiveness. The open-network structure is feasible with the implementation of an integrated performance measurement system and stakeholder pay.

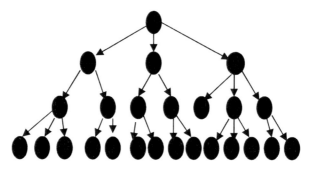

Conventional Bureaucratic System

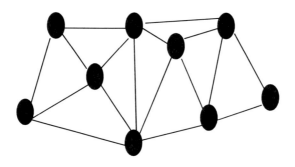

Open Network System

Organizational Advantages of an Open Network System
- Responsive to external events
- Nimble, ability to change rapidly
- Continuous improvement
- Customer focus
- Profit focus
- Resilient and sustainable

Employee Advantages of an Open Network System

- feel free . . . doing what they *want* to do
- may be fewer unwanted by-products
- behavior shaped by nonsocial contingencies is as universal as the contingencies
- contingency-shaped behavior is likely to be hot and Epicurean, more likely to be associated with joy
- likely to have a greater variety or richness
- contingencies contain reasons which rules can never specify (B.F. Skinner, 1969)

Closed vs. Open Systems

Systems theory recognizes that the interdependence between groups of individuals, structures, and processes enables an organization to function. It is recognized that organizations are complex social systems. The interactions between employees and their organizational environments are seen as the target of analysis and management.

The systems theorist Ludwig von Bertalanffy, described the differences between open and closed systems. A closed system is unresponsive to events outside the system while an open system adapts to changes outside the system. An *open system* is defined as follows:

A system with input, an entity that changes its behavior in response to conditions outside its boundaries. Systems are rarely ever either open or closed but open to some and closed to other influences. Adaptation, learning and all manifestations of intelligence require some openness to information. (Von Bertalanffy, 1968)

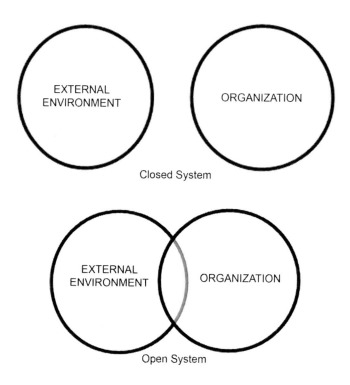

Closed systems are insulated from the external environment (meta-system) in which they operate. As long as the metasystem remains constant, the closed system functions relatively effectively. However, if there are changes in the metasystem, the closed system is not adaptive and becomes dysfunctional.

Evolution of Closed Behavior Systems

In the beginning, most business organizations are open systems that adapt and change to dynamic business conditions external to the organization. As organizations grow in size and complexity, the emerging hierarchy and subsystems often function more and more as closed systems. John Case, in his *Open-Book Management* states the following:

> *As the industrial economy matured, American companies creat-*
> *ed a new paradigm of management. They institutionalized and*
> *routinized their management methods. They developed practic-*
> *es and procedures that came to be taken for granted in the*
> *business world. It took maybe half a century for all the pieces to*
> *fall into place. But these two ideas – that jobs must be special-*
> *ized and that employees need close supervision – were always*
> *at the heart of the system. (Case, 1995)*

Case attributed this movement toward closed systems within the organization to the rise of Frederick Taylor's scientific management, the professionalization of management, and the rise of the adversarial union.

The Emergence of Aversive Control

Before Henry Ford introduced large-scale job specialization, small teams of craftsmen assembled automobiles (and many other products). These craftsmen produced the final product and were paid directly for it. In this direct provider-customer relationship, on-time delivery and product quality directly impacted the workers. As organizations grew larger and more complex, the assembly line and job specialization were introduced. Job specialization often increased organizational productivity, but severed the natural connection between the worker, his product, and his pay.

Job specialization also contributed to the shift away from pay for results to the wage-and-salary system. Organizations that introduced job specialization found it difficult to measure and monitor individual employee results and pay for them. When pay shifted to fixed wages, pay was no longer effective as a positive reinforcer for employee performance. This made it necessary to substantially increase the level of direct supervision. Many of Henry Ford's management practices were developed and promoted by Frederick Taylor, the founder of Scientific Management. Taylor recommended an astonishingly tight (and expensive) ratio of one supervisor for every four workers.

Pay for performance was replaced with direct supervision. Job specialization also removed many of the natural positive consequences derived from the successful completion of a finished product. This meant that the manager or supervisor, at every level of the organization, had to find another way to ensure subordinates performed. The alternative was aversive control. Pay for performance (positive reinforcement) was replaced with subtle—and not so subtle—intimidation and fear (negative reinforcement).

B. F. Skinner (1969) explained the difference in this way:

Historically, people have been controlled primarily through negative reinforcement. That is, they have been punished when they have not done what is reinforcing to those who could punish them. Positive reinforcement has been less often used, partly because the effect is slightly deferred, but it can be as effective as negative reinforcement and has many fewer unwanted by-products.

Organizations that rely on aversive control (punishment and intimidation) of employees must, necessarily, devolve to closed systems. For example, dictatorships, which rely heavily on aversive control, consistently attempt to limit information flow through control of the press and travel restrictions. One extreme case was the wall the Soviet Union built around itself. In a speech, John F. Kennedy remarked, "We are not afraid to entrust the American people with unpleasant facts, foreign ideas, alien philosophies, and competitive values. For a nation that is afraid to let its people judge the truth and falsehood in an open market is a nation that is afraid of its people."

The paranoia dictators demonstrate with regard to their subjects also exists for owners and managers of organizations that rely heavily on aversive control. Market conditions, strategies, financial information and salary assignments are closely guarded and not shared with employees. Organizations that rely on aversive control do not share information with employees nor do they often allow them the discretion to innovate upon information they do receive.

Aversive control thrives on ambiguity and a sense of helplessness. When we think of situations in which aversive control is used, visions of slavery and sweatshops come to mind. Unfortunately, aversive control is often much less obvious than this. One reason it is difficult to see aversive control is that it prompts avoidance behavior and, if effective, the sanctions are rarely actually applied. In fact, a management group that is really effective at intimidation will rarely have to apply sanctions. Put simply, in many, if not most organizations, employees work to avoid aversive sanctions.

Other Deficiencies of Aversive Control

In addition to the disadvantages of a closed system, there are three other important reasons for the organization to shift from traditional aversive control to a greater reliance on positive reinforcement.

First, aversive control undermines employee morale and job satisfaction. Operationally, these translate to grievances, uncooperativeness, attendance problems, and attrition. B.F. Skinner (1969) wrote the following:

> *Those who respond because their behavior has had positively reinforcing consequences usually **feel** free. They seem to be doing what they **want** to do. Those who respond because the reinforcement has been negative and who are therefore avoiding or escaping from punishment are doing what they **have** to do and do not feel free.*

Second, negative reinforcement fails to produce optimal performance levels. Regarding the effects of negative reinforcement, Daniels and Bailey (2014) wrote as follows:

The problem is that once the consequence has been avoided, there is no motivation to do more. As long as the person does enough to keep the negative consequence from happening, his behavior has reached its objective.

Third, coercion may produce counter control. "Instead of acting in accord with controlling conditions, controlees sometimes counter control; that is, they oppose controlling attempts by moving out of range, attacking, or passively resisting" (Delprato, 2002). Organizational examples of moving out of range include absenteeism, tardiness, extended breaks, and ultimately, quitting. Organizational examples of attacking include complaints, arguments, rumors, sabotage, and physical confrontations. Passive resistance may be in the form of failing to carry out assignments or intentional inaccuracy or delays.

Time for a Change

The conventional wage-and-salary system creates closed, bureaucratic performance systems that are inflexible and unresponsive to environmental changes. The system constrains employee performance, initiative, and organizational commitment. It requires expensive, direct supervision and prompts counter control.

The conventional system evolved from changes in technology—especially the introduction of the assembly line. Today, the assembly line applies to only a small fraction of organizations. Early manufacturing environments could function relatively well as closed systems due to the ready availability of a stable, full-time work force and minimal competition. The general stability of the business environment in that era is quite different than today's rapid changes in technology, international competition, and customer and employee demands. Direct supervision is no longer a viable option for virtual organizations that employ contractors, outsourcing and telecommuting, or that operate with diverse, multiple locations that may span several continents.

References

Arrow, H., McGrath, J.E. & Berdahl, J.L. (2000). *Small Groups as Complex Systems*. Thousand Oaks, CA: Sage Publications.

Case, J. (1995). *Open-Book Management*. New York: HarperCollins Books.

Cramer, F. (1993). *Chaos and Order,* New York: VCH

Daniels, A. C., Bailey, J. S. (2014). *Performance Management: Changing Behavior that Drives Organizational Effectiveness.* Atlanta, GA: Performance Management Publications.

Delprato, D. J. (2002) Contercontrol in behavior analysis. *The Behavior Analyst*, 2: 192.

Ellis, W. D. (1938). *Source Book of Gestalt Psychology.* New York: Harcourt, Brace and Co.

Skinner, B.F. (1969). *Contingencies of Reinforcement: A Theoretical Analysis*. New York: Meredith Corporation.

Von Bertalanffy, L. (1968). *General System Theory: Foundations, Development, Applications.* New York: George Braziller, revised edition 1976.

Chapter 5

Utopian Visions

In 1948, B.F. Skinner published *Walden Two. Walden Two* was a utopian novel that described a community designed around Skinner's **positive reinforcement**. He later expanded his ideas on designing cultures in *Science and Human Behavior* (1953), *Contingencies of Reinforcement: A Theoretical Analysis* (1969), and *Beyond Freedom and Dignity* (1971). In the 1960s and early '70s there were a number of attempts to apply the *Walden Two* concepts including Walden House, 1969; Lake Village, 1971; Los Horcones, 1971; and the Twin Oaks Community, 1974. Some of these applications failed while others moved to modified versions of *Walden Two*.

Skinner argued for developing utopian principles and techniques in smaller settings. The fictional *Walden Two* had a population similar to that of a medium-sized company—approximately 1,000 members. In his introduction to the 1976 printing of *Walden Two*, Skinner further stressed this point.

If we want to find out how people can live together without quarreling, can produce the goods they need without working too hard, or can raise and educate their children more efficiently, let us start with units of manageable size before moving on to larger units. (p. ix, Skinner, 1976)

For those of us interested in improving the human condition, rather than attempting large-scale social changes, we should consider Skinner's advice and begin with existing organizations. Existing business organizations are a promising utopian alternative. These organizations are already economically viable and have an identity and a political structure based on private, public, or employee ownership. If these organizations operated on sound behavioral principles, a more limited form of utopia would be achieved for working people. As these practices thrive, it is possible they would then spread to the society at large.

A quick review of utopian concepts and problems can be instructive to the manager or owner who is considering a new approach to managing the workplace. The word *utopia* translates from the Latin as *no place land* and was coined by Sir Thomas More in 1515. A utopian community and utopian thinkers are defined in the *New Lexicon Webster's Dictionary* as follows:

Any imaginary political and social system in which relationships between individuals and the state are perfectly adjusted

Someone who believes in the immediate perfectibility of human society by the application of some idealistic scheme

Notable historical examples of utopian proposals were Plato's *Republic*, Augustine's *The City of God*, Thomas More's *Utopia*, Francis Bacon's *The New Atlantis*, William Morris' *News from Nowhere*, and Edward Bellamy's *Looking Backward*. The utopian vision is also expressed in mythology, as for example, Arcadia and Shangri-La.

Utopian communities have been organized on political principles (Greece's Sparta), religious principles (the Shaker Movement), and scientific and technological principles (Buckminster Fuller's vision). They have often been organized around economic principles as, for example, Edward Bellamy's, *Looking Backward*. The Soviet Union was, in this sense, an economic utopian community. Generally, the goal of economic utopias is a more equitable distribution of goods and services. Consequently, the majority of these communities adopted some variation of socialism. As a reaction to the expansion of capitalism, almost one hundred utopian communities were founded in the United States from 1805 to 1855 (Jacoby, 2005).

The historical failure rate of utopian communities has been severe. In some cases these failures were due to leadership or conflicts among various factions. There are also many examples of commune failures due to the fact they simply could not sustain themselves economically. Many utopian communities failed because they were closed systems. As a result, aversive and dysfunctional practices often evolved. These problems can also affect businesses seeking a new management strategy. Business organizations, however, are less likely to become closed systems because to survive they must interact with customers, vendors, competitors, and the government.

Issues with Socialism and Profit Sharing

In socialist utopias, the community's goods and services are distributed equally among the members with little regard for individual contributions. Socialism was the early economic system of the Pilgrims. The results were disastrous and the community came close to extinction. Members were then allowed to keep most of what they produced while sharing a percentage of their production with the community (a tax). Under this system, the community prospered.

Socialism has a fatal design flaw in that the distributions of goods and services are not contingent on individual member contributions. Consequently, individual productivity suffers. Another serious flaw in socialist income distribution schemes is what economists term the *free rider effect*. Some people simply fail to contribute their fair share of goods or services to the community. The business parallel to socialist communities is a profit-sharing program in which each employee receives an equal share of annual excess profits. Many businesses view profit sharing as an example of pay for performance. However, just as in socialism, each employee typically receives an equal share regardless of contribution.

Issues with Management and Supervision

Skinner's utopian vision makes no mention of conventional supervisors. In *Walden Two*, Skinner repeatedly refers to behavioral engineering and behavior engineers. One can interpret Skinner as arguing that organizations should eliminate the supervisor functions and replace them with direct payments for individual and team contributions to the organization.

> *You can't foresee all future circumstances. You don't know what will be required. Instead, you have to set up certain behavioral processes which will lead the individual to design his own "good conduct" when the time comes. (Skinner, p. 105, 1969)*

Bureaucratic management often devolves to aversive control. In its place, we should work toward self-managed employees or employee teams who are in direct contact with the results of their efforts. These individuals or teams would voluntarily request the service of manager/facilitators to assist them in coordinating across departments and removing performance constraints inherent in any organization's performance system.

Skinner also refers to planners throughout *Walden Two*. In *The Liberated Workplace,* planners are needed to connect the employee teams to the outside environment. Planners analyze consumer preferences, economic changes, resources, governmental regulations, competition, and changes in technology. Based on these analyses they design performance measures for employees and change these performance measures and priorities as their market analyses dictate. They don't serve as traditional managers nor have any direct command-and-control authority. Employee-owned companies or employee stock options would do much to diffuse potential abuses of power by planners. That is, the planners would not be the sole owners.

Once the planners' strategy is communicated through performance measures, day-to-day management would be performed by the self-managed employee teams. Facilitators would provide on-call assistance to the teams. The facilitators would also integrate job descriptions, employee selection, and training with the performance-measurement system. Traditional performance evaluations would no longer be relevant.

Throughout *Walden Two*, Skinner makes the case for creating more free time for employees. In Skinner's *Walden Two*, people only worked four hours a day. In some organizations there may be limits on how much revenue can be generated. In these cases, improvements in efficiency would enable employees to work shorter hours or fewer days. For customer contact jobs that require full-time staffing of eight hours (customer service, nursing, et cetera), job sharing could be used to distribute free time. Providing employees more free time does not increase the cost of doing business if the employees produce the same amount of goods or services within the reduced hours.

   The difference is, we get rid of the work, not the worker. (p. 76, Skinner, 1948)

The management system to be described borrows from Skinner's *Walden Two* the concepts of planners, facilitators, direct payment for performance, and self-managed employees.

References

Jacoby, Russell. (2005). *Picture Imperfect: Utopian Thought for an Anti-Utopian Age*. New York: Columbia University Press.

Skinner, B.F. (1948, 1976, 2005). *Walden Two*. Indianapolis: Hackett Publishing Company.

Skinner, B.F. (1953). *Science and Human Behavior*. New York: The Free Press.

Skinner, B.F. (1969). *Contingencies of Reinforcement: A Theoretical Analysis*. New York: Meredith Corporation.

Skinner, B.F. (1971). *Beyond Freedom and Dignity*. New York: Bantam Vintage.

Skinner, B.F. (1987). *Upon Further Reflection*. New York: Prentice Hall.

Chapter 6

Transition Strategy
Toward a Liberated Workplace

Transition Levels Toward a Liberated Workplace

Level IV: Self-Management
Results: Commitment & Independence

Reduced Supervision Expense
Reduced Turnover

Level III: Job Enrichment
Results: Consistent Opportunity, Flexibility, Engagement

Improved Productivity
Increased Responsiveness

Level II: Stakeholder Pay
Results: High Earnings Opportunity, Job Security

Affordable Payroll

Level I: Scorecards, Positive Leadership, Facilitation
Results: Improved Management, Performance, & Morale

Improved Performance

Over many implementations, a transition strategy has developed for moving an organization from the conventional bureaucratic, pay-for-time performance system to a self-managed, pay-for-results performance system. The strategy consists of four levels the organization moves through, beginning with a results focus and moving to self-managed teams.

Conventional Workplace

The conventional workplace refers to an organization that utilizes a bureaucratic management system; pays its employees a wage or salary; conducts subjective performance reviews; and uses these reviews to determine annual merit pay increases and promotions. It is this performance system that is the target of the transition strategy toward a liberated workplace. The following transition stages are referred to as levels because an organization may elect to stop the transition at any level short of a true, liberated workplace.

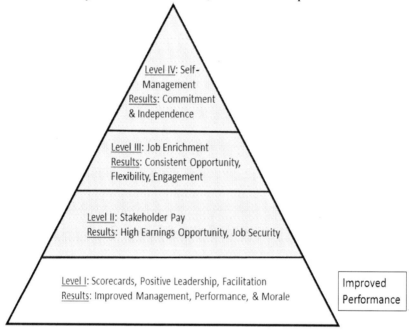

Level IV: Self-Management
Results: Commitment & Independence

Level III: Job Enrichment
Results: Consistent Opportunity, Flexibility, Engagement

Level II: Stakeholder Pay
Results: High Earnings Opportunity, Job Security

Level I: Scorecards, Positive Leadership, Facilitation
Results: Improved Management, Performance, & Morale

Improved Performance

LEVEL I

Level I: Results Focus

The first level consists of implementing an organization-wide performance measurement system. The performance measurement system serves as the basis for a performance improvement program. Specific scorecard measures for each job position are selected as targets for performance improvement projects. Improvements are reinforced through one-time bonuses to the managers and their subordinates. This level also includes the administration of the Leadership Survey to identify, train, and coach managers who experience difficulty in making the transition to positive management. Level I can be the final level for an organization that simply wants to improve leadership and targeted performances. It may also serve as a launchpad for the organization's transition to Level II.

Results Measurement

The first step in the development of a liberated organization's performance system is the design and implementation of an organization-wide performance measurement system. It may seem incongruous that the first step in liberating employees is to introduce performance measurement. However, objective performance measurement frees the employee from conventional aversive control and time-centered management.

Measure Actionable Results. The measurement system should track results that are directly actionable through changes in employee behavior. Results that depend upon large or diverse groups of employees do not meet this criterion. For example, the profit of the organization involves employees in many areas. This result is too removed from any one employee to be effective in managing behavior (except in a very small organization).

Measure All Key Results. Why track all key employee results? Why not simply track problem results? Three reasons are as follows:

- In the absence of a comprehensive results measurement system, it is difficult to identify which results most require intervention.
- Many results are interdependent and interventions with respect to one result may have an adverse impact on other key results. This interaction will not be known if only problem results are monitored.
- If only problem results are measured and reinforced through the performance pay system, then other key results may be ignored by employees and become

problems themselves. The objective of an effective measurement system is a balanced improvement across all key results.

Measurement Categories. How are valid performance measures for a job position determined? Does the diversity of types and sizes of organizations create a problem? It is true that at the process level each organization is unique. Fortunately, there are many similarities between organizations at the financial level. If this were not so, general accounting practices would be impossible. With respect to financial outcomes, four classes of financial results are commonly impacted by employees (Abernathy, 2011). These are the generation of revenues, expense control, productivity (payroll expenses), and cash flow (collections, inventory, & payables).

There are also three non-financial categories: regulatory compliance, customer service, and developmental projects. Regulatory compliance measures are grouped for convenience according to regulatory agencies (such as OSHA, DOT, EPA, FDA, and so on). Customer-service measures are often not tracked in conventional financial reporting and include product or service accuracy, timeliness, and customer-service ratings. Finally, developmental projects are not tracked in an organization's financials and project progress and quality have to be tracked independently. These three non-financial categories are typically tracked as lead indicators where financial indicators are tracked as lag indicators. For examples, in addition to compliance errors, compliance audits and compliant behavioral observations are tracked. Similarly, customer service surveys warn in advance of potential customer attrition. Finally, projects are typically measured in milestones rather than simply the completion of the project.

The four financial measure categories relate to short-term profitability while the three non-financial categories relate more to long-term profitability. Using these seven categories to define performance measures substantially reduces the development time of a measurement system. Each organization's executive group defines and prioritizes the category measures in terms of their impact on their unique organization's strategy. To develop performance measures for lower-level job positions only requires determining which of the measurement categories the job position affects.

The Performance Matrix

The performance matrix or objectives matrix (Felix & Riggs, 1986) format is used for organizing multiple performance measures and balancing their relative priorities into a scorecard. The matrix specifies a priority weighted percentage—a min and max—for each measure. We have adapted the matrix terms *base* and *goal,* for profit-indexed performance pay purposes, to *min* and *max*. The min represents current, average, or minimum acceptable level of performance. The max represents the performance level at which maximum incentive opportunity is achieved. Each reporting period, the percent gain (actual-min / max-min) is computed for each measure which converts the measures to a common scale. This percent gain is then multiplied by the priority weight to compute a weighted percent gain. Finally, these weighted percent gains are summed to compute an overall performance index. This performance index represents the employee's overall priority weighed performance. The performance matrix mathematically ensures balanced performance and provides a convenient format for performance measurement across the organization.

Performance Scales													
MEASURE NAME	-20	-10	MIN 0	10	20	30	40	50	60	80	MAX 100	WT	WTD SCORE
Gross Revenue	$15,000	$20,000	$25,000	$30,000	$35,000	$40,000	$45,000	$50,000	$55,000	$60,000	$65,000	20%	-4.0
Gross Margin %	9.0%	9.5%	10.0%	10.5%	11.0%	11.5%	12.0%	12.5%	13.0%	13.5%	14.0%	20%	0.0
% Project Milestones	50%	55%	60%	65%	70%	75%	80%	85%	90%	95%	100%	40%	20.0
Customer Survey	4.0	4.5	5.0	5.5	6.0	6.5	7.0	7.5	8.0	8.5	9.0	0%	20.0
											Performance Index		36.0

Aligning Key Results

What process is used to identify key results throughout the organization? Since the ultimate goal of the performance system is to improve organizational performance, the measurement process should begin at the organizational level rather than at the job level. This method of designing a measurement system is termed *the method of cascading objectives.*

Using cascading objectives, key strategic results are first defined for the organization. These results guide the development of measures for senior managers, middle managers, and continue down to the worker level. This procedure ensures all measures drive the organizational strategy because each designer will logically develop subordinate measures that positively impact on his or her higher-level measures. In addition to alignment, another advantage of this top-down approach is it proves to be much more efficient in developing an enterprise-wide measurement system than does a bottom-up measurement strategy (Abernathy, 2011).

Performance Pay

Many types of performance pay schemes are available. These include variations of commission, piece-rate, goal-sharing, gain-sharing, and profit-sharing plans. The economist, Martin Weitzman (1984), described the benefits of replacing wages and salaries with profit sharing. Through many years of field applications of the various performance pay plans, the author has arrived at a plan that best meets the needs of an enterprise-wide performance system. The plan is termed Profit-Indexed Performance Pay (PIPP), (Abernathy, 2011). PIPP determines each employee's performance pay opportunity based upon the profitability of the organization. This opportunity is expressed as a percentage of each employee's base pay. The greater the organization's profitability, the higher is the employee performance pay opportunity percentage.

The second step is to index these profit shares to personal and/or team performance. That is, the profit share is indexed to employee scorecard performance. Indexing profit shares serves three purposes. First, indexing ensures that performance pay is always affordable for the organization. When profits are very low, the index moves near zero and little performance pay opportunity is available. When profits are high, the index enables a high percentage, above-market, potential of base pay. The second purpose of indexing is to ensure the measurement system is self-correcting. If the performance measures are incorrectly identified, improvements in these performances will not increase profits, and employee performance pay opportunity is lowered. Third, indexing profit shares to the performance scorecards ensures that profits are fairly distributed to those employees who contributed the most.

In PIPP the performance pay opportunity is determined by the organization's profit. However, each employee, employee team, or a mix of personal and team measures, produces a matrix performance index or scorecard score that determines how much of the available profit share for the month is awarded. PIPP is not general profit sharing since each employee's performance pay earnings are determined by their actual performances. On the other hand, neither is PIPP goal sharing or a commission or piece-rate plan, since performance pay opportunity is determined by overall profitability rather than guaranteed.

PIPP Performance Pay Calculation

Assigned Performance Pay Opportunity %		Profit Multiplier		Performance Pay Opportunity %		Individual's Performance Index %		Performance Payout of Base Pay
10 %	X	1.5	=	15 %	X	60 %	=	9 %

In this above example, the employee is assigned a performance pay opportunity percentage of 10 percent of his base pay. In the current month, profits are sufficient enough that the assigned opportunity percentage can be increased by 1.5 to 15 percent. The employee's personal or team performance index on his matrix is 60 percent. The 15 percent opportunity is multiplied by the employee's performance index to yield an actual payout of 9 percent of his monthly salary or hourly earnings.

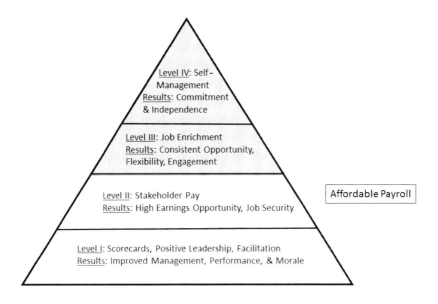

LEVEL II

Level II: Stakeholder Pay

Level II replaces the performance improvement bonuses in Level I with *Profit-Indexed Performance Pay* (PIPP). PIPP is implemented across the organization based upon the performance scorecards implemented in Level I.

PIPP can be a permanent performance pay plan that offers market-based wages and salaries plus a modest monthly or quarterly bonus based upon profitability and individual or small-team performance. However, employees who receive a modest performance pay opportunity, in addition to a market-competitive base pay, are not true stakeholders in the organization. When employees are paid a guaranteed wage or salary equivalent to what other companies pay, they are taking no risk with the introduction of performance pay. There is no *motivating operation* to change their behavior. Put simply, an employee can sleep through the program and still receive the same pay he or she would receive at another company.

The author has been successful with several client organizations in implementing stakeholder pay or pay-at-risk. Two strategies have been employed to move employees from market-comparable base pay to below-market base pay plus performance pay. The first conversion strategy is to substitute an increase in PIPP performance pay opportunity for the conventional merit and cost-of-living annual base pay increase. This change will gradually index more employee pay to profitability and personal performance and less to a guaranteed wage or salary.

The second strategy is a voluntary base-pay reduction in exchange for an increase in performance pay opportunity. Of course, the employee must receive an adequate return-on-investment for that portion of base pay put at risk. In applications, a three-to-one, risk-reward ratio has been used successfully. That is, for every dollar the employee puts at risk, an additional three-dollar performance pay opportunity is provided. Put another way, a 10 percent reduction in base pay is offset by a 20 percent of base pay performance pay earnings opportunity.

Some employees have volunteered for pay-at-risk in every client organization that has made the offer. Typically, only a few volunteer in the beginning. As they are successful, other employees follow their lead. To further illustrate the potential for stakeholder pay, on several occasions during the installation of the no-risk phase of performance pay, employees have proposed that they would take a risk (base-pay reduction) for a greater share of the profits—even though no such option had been presented!

I worked with a large, unionized manufacturing company. Management had decided to build another plant that manufactured something new to the organization. After much discussion, they decided to open the new plant offering wages 15 percent below wages at their other plants, which were in nearby locations. In exchange for the pay reduction, employees could earn up to 30 percent above the average pay in the other plants if the plant met profitability targets.

The managers were concerned that no one would volunteer so they held a meeting where employees could learn about the plan. The meeting had much higher attendance than expected. I returned home and in a few weeks received a phone call from one of the managers. The concern had been that no one would volunteer, but the fact was that they had more volunteers than job openings!

When proposing stakeholder pay, many client managers argue that lower-paid hourly employees would not want to participate. In fact, the opposite is usually the case. High-paid, salaried workers have more invested in their pay than do lower-paid, hourly workers. This investment includes education, experience, and the effort invested in obtaining promotions. The hourly worker has less such investment. This lack of investment by the lower-paid employee also severely restricts their future earnings potential. To earn a good living, stakeholder pay may be the only viable option for low-paid employees. The table below summarizes the differences between conventional entitlement pay and stakeholder pay.

Entitlement Pay	vs.	Stakeholder Pay
• Pay for time • Direct supervision • Pay range set by market • Performance-based promotions • Company does not share profit gains in good times and lays off employees in bad times		• Pay for results • Facilitation • Pay range set by profit and performance • No cap on earnings in each job • Company shares profit gains and can provide lifetime employment in a fully leveraged stakeholder pay system

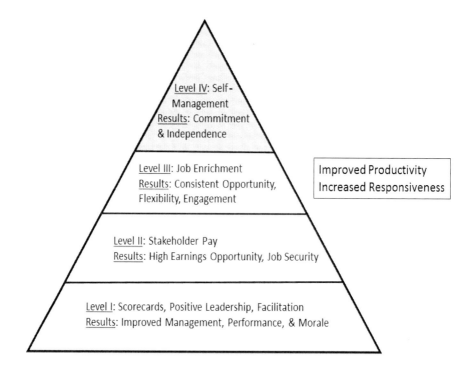

LEVEL III

Level III: Job Enrichment

Level III is introduced most effectively after Level II, stakeholder pay has been introduced. This is because in Level II the employee directly shares in the organization's business risks and rewards. To ensure high and consistent performance pay earnings, employees will need to move to Level IIII by expanding their job skills, taking on more decision-making responsibility, and optimizing their work schedules.

The first step in Level III is to institute an organization-wide hiring freeze. As employees leave the organization, the remaining employees have a chance to maximize their performance pay earnings by taking on some of the duties of employees who left. The second step is to reinforce the manager for facilitating job enrichment tactics by adding a team productivity measure to the manager's scorecard. Five job enrichment strategies are available for improving individual and team productivity. These are as follows:

1. *Job enlargement*—The number of assigned job functions is increased to ensure sufficient work input and to reduce the number of unique job positions.

2. *Employee empowerment*—Decision-making authority for selected processes are transferred from the manager to the subordinate. This enables the worker to process work with fewer delays.

3. *Flexible scheduling*—Employees agree to part-time work arrival and departure times based upon input volume cycles. Since pay is determined by performance, the net result is no reduction in pay but a reduction in work hours.

4. *Work prospecting*—During low, work-input periods, additional work is brought into the department from other areas or outside of the organization.

5. *Cross-utilization*— During low, work-input periods, employees work in areas outside the department. This strategy involves cross-training employees.

Lateral Career Paths

The more skills each employee possesses, the less disruptive are unanticipated volume surges or employee absences. Consequently, organizations that highly prize these benefits may increase an employee's performance pay opportunity in recognition of learning additional skills and increasing personal value to the enterprise. This practice is termed *lateral career paths*. That is, employees can increase their performance pay opportunity by laterally learning new skills rather than vertical promotions to management. Employees no longer have to enter management to increase their earnings. However, it is important to note that the employee's performance pay opportunity is increased—not necessarily their actual earnings. They must actually perform the enriched activities to receive payment.

A criticism of the creation of a flat organization is that employee career paths are eliminated. The conventional vision of moving up through the organization, and perhaps becoming an executive, is constrained by a flat organization. If the sole reason for moving up the hierarchy is more money, stakeholder pay provides this opportunity in much the way as it is provided to a self-employed individual. Self-employed people are never promoted—they expand their services or products to make more money, increase job security, or have more free time.

Another concern is that the removal of the promotion hierarchy presents a less interesting and challenging career. In the liberated workplace, lateral career paths replace vertical career paths. Rather than moving up the organization, the ambitious employee moves across the organization by cross-training and working in other functions.

This approach harkens back to the 1960s when job enlargement and job enrichment became popular management ideas. The problem, then, was the assumption that employees would want to cross-train simply to make their jobs more interesting. In retrospect, this proved a rather weak benefit for many employees. More work and responsibility, without additional compensation, was a bad bargain for the employee.

In the Stakeholder Pay System, the more jobs you learn to perform, the greater and more consistent is your performance pay. This is particularly the case in organizations that have complex work-input cycles. The well cross-trained individual can simply move to where the work is. As more employees become involved, a second major benefit is the need for fewer employees which increases profitability and Profit-Indexed Performance Pay without sacrificing the organization's responsiveness.

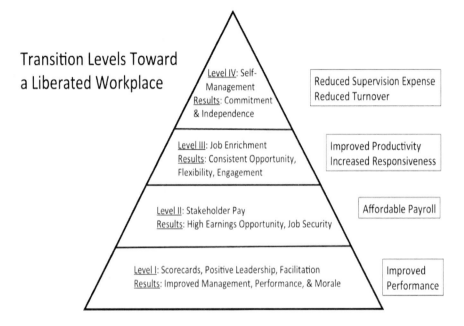

Transition Levels Toward a Liberated Workplace

Level IV: Self-Management
Results: Commitment & Independence

Reduced Supervision Expense
Reduced Turnover

Level III: Job Enrichment
Results: Consistent Opportunity, Flexibility, Engagement

Improved Productivity
Increased Responsiveness

Level II: Stakeholder Pay
Results: High Earnings Opportunity, Job Security

Affordable Payroll

Level I: Scorecards, Positive Leadership, Facilitation
Results: Improved Management, Performance, & Morale

Improved Performance

LEVEL IV

Level IV: Self-Managed Teams

Levels I and II establish the foundation for a liberated workplace. Level III removes work availability constraints that would undermine the transition. However, more work must be done to create a truly liberated workplace. This final step is to move toward self-managed teams and individuals. A key strategy for moving to self-management is to increase the manager span of control.

Span of control is the ratio of workers to managers and can also be thought of in reverse as the self-management ratio. The self-management ratio improves as the number of managers relative to the number of workers decreases. Organizations with excessive numbers of managers and supervisors restrict the liberated approach to management in several ways. First, the greater the number of non-producing employees (managers), the smaller the Profit-Indexed Performance Pay is to the producers. Second, the greater the number of management levels, the more restricted are employees in responding to external and internal environmental changes. Third, and perhaps most important, the path of least effort for supervisors is always aversive control. A truly liberated workplace minimizes aversive control and maximizes positive reinforcement. Only with the elimination of close supervision can employees act and feel truly liberated.

An unfortunate consequence of the introduction of the conventional wage-and-salary system was a reduction in the manager's ability to financially recognize good performance. What has replaced direct financial incentives is the promotion. It has become a common practice to promote good performers into management positions as a reward for their contributions as workers. This unfortunate event has created organizations with swollen bureaucracies.

The first tactic to increase span of control is to put a halt to the practice of using promotions as rewards for good performance. Promotions to management will only occur when a management/facilitator position is truly needed, and only individuals who are interested in management and have the requisite skills are offered the position. The lateral career paths described in Level III replace the conventional bureaucratic vertical career paths.

A second tactic is to increase the performance pay opportunity of managers based upon the number of people and the complexity of the jobs they manage. Two concerns here are that managers increase their span of control by simply hiring more employees, or that they fail to provide their subordinates effective performance facilitation. Fortunately, the performance pay system is designed to counteract these issues. Simply adding employees will reduce the manager's productivity ratio on his performance scorecard. If a manager fails to facilitate, the roll-up performance of their subordinates will decrease which, in turn, decreases the manager's performance pay.

As manager span of control increases, the ability to micromanage subordinates decreases and day-to-day decision authority naturally and necessarily shifts to the workers. The manager's role changes from supervising to facilitating. Facilitation includes managing budgets, coordinating activities with other departments, vendors, and customers, and removing individual and team performance constraints through improving work opportunity, capability, and context.

References

Abernathy, W.B. (2011). *Pay for Profit: Creating an Organization-wide Performance System.* Atlanta: Performance Management Publications.

Felix, G.H. and Riggs, J.L. (1986). *Productivity by the Objectives Matrix.* Corvalis, OR: Oregon Productivity Center.

Weitzman, M. L. (1984). *The Share Economy: Conquering Stagflation.* Boston: Harvard University Press.

Section II:

A Liberated Workplace

Chapter 7

Superior Button

The following is a case study of a hypothetical organization's transition toward a liberated workplace.

My name is Sid Murray. I am an entrepreneur whose primary business is a factory—Superior Button—that manufactures buttons for dress shirts and blouses. I solely own the factory and have been in business for over 15 years. The factory employs around 100 people.

During the past three years Superior Button has seen a steady decline in profits. For the first time in the company's history, I am seriously considering a lay-off of some of my employees. I have always been a generous and fair-minded employer, so I am quite upset about my situation and anxious about my impending decisions.

"I don't know what I'm going to do," I said to my chief financial officer, Margaret, and my human resources director, Julie. "I won't even be able to cover our loan payments if our profit drops much more."

Margaret responded, "The problem is our margin. It just keeps shrinking and shrinking."

"Tell me again what's causing the margin problem?" I asked.

"Well, we have a lot of fixed costs that are increasing each year, even though our sales volume stays about the same," Margaret explained.

I asked, "What kinds of fixed costs are you talking about?"

Margaret thought a minute and said, "The basic materials expense has remained about the same, though our scrap rate is still too high.

But, the main problem is employee expenses including payroll and benefits. Our employee expense used to be around 26 percent of our revenue—now it's up to 42 percent and still climbing!"

Margaret's comment visibly upset Julie, the HR director. Julie blurted out, "I don't know how this can be! We are paying competitive compensation and only giving 3 to 4 percent annual increases. We could cut back on benefits, but I'm afraid we would have a mass exodus."

I said curtly, "We're going to have a mass exodus anyway if things remain the same."

I decided to talk directly to my employees to see if things could be improved before more drastic actions had to be taken. I began with the sales staff first. My five salespeople were paid generous salaries plus a small commission on each sale. They had all been with me a while. The sales meeting was held in a conference room at a local restaurant. All five salespeople showed up on time. I brought along my CFO, Margaret, for support. Everyone knew each other and they spent some time catching up on each other's personal lives. No one, except Margaret, was aware of what the meeting was about.

I began, somewhat nervously, "I called this meeting to update everyone on our financial situation. If you'll look at the handouts you will see that our total sales have declined 5 percent over the past three years and our gross margin has dropped from 12 percent to 7 percent. Even worse, our labor expense keeps increasing and our profit is down almost 40 percent!"

Elaine had joined Superior Button right out of college three years ago. She was our best salesperson but she was sometimes painfully direct in any discussion. "Why are you telling us this?" Elaine asked in an accusing voice.

I responded, "If things don't improve by April, we will have to lay off a lot of employees."

Elaine said, "I don't think it's fair for you to make sure you make a profit by getting rid of people who have been loyal to your company for many years. They all have families and bills to pay!"

I was flabbergasted and angry. "I have to make a living just like you do!" I said loudly. Some of my family members are investors who put their own money in the company and deserve a reasonable return on those investments."

Elaine was not deterred. "Of course, but do you guys have to make it at the expense of the workers?" she asked.

I replied, "I tell you what Elaine, would you be willing to take a cut in pay to prevent some of the workers from being laid off?"

Elaine was getting really agitated. "I don't make enough as it is! Why should I have to take a pay cut just because the company isn't doing well? It's not my fault and it isn't fair."

I belatedly began to realize that Elaine, and probably most of the other employees, did not understand, or didn't want to understand, how their performances impacted the overall profit of the company. She truly felt she was entitled to her pay regardless of the overall financial health of Superior Button. It was as though Elaine thought there was a black box from which salaries were drawn and that this black box had an infinite reserve, regardless of profits.

Part of the problem was that I had never shared financial information with the employees. I felt it was none of the employees' business how much management made and that if I did tell the employees they would likely want more money. I wondered how I could get my employees as concerned about company profit as I was. How could they work *with* management rather than as adversaries? I didn't have the answers, so I decided now wasn't the time for Business 101. Instead, I directed the discussion specifically to sales issues.

"We can prevent the layoffs if we improve our sales," I said, ignoring Elaine's accusation. "As I said, gross sales are down and our gross margin is really down. Do you guys have any idea why?"

John had been with the company longer than any other salesperson. He didn't like confrontation, especially with me, but felt he should answer the question. "We are all working hard. Our customer orders have been declining over the past several years. When I talk to them, they tell me our prices are in line, but that we don't turn around their orders quickly enough. Because of this, they are beginning to use other suppliers," he said.

I replied, "What about getting more new customers?"

John said, "We've called on most of the prospects and they keep telling us they are satisfied with the suppliers they already have."

I asked, "How many prospects are there in our five-state sales region?"

Without much conviction, John stated, "Well, we really don't have very good marketing data, but I would guess around 300."

"How often have they been called on?" I asked.

Bob, who was sitting at the end of the table, spoke up, "We call on all the prospects regularly and they are just not interested."

"Let's be specific," I said. "How many prospects are there and how many times a year is each prospect visited?"

I was startled by the blank looks around the table. It was obvious that no one really knew. I remembered that a few years ago they had discussed tracking weekly sales calls, but had decided it was just too much trouble. After all, at that point the company was doing pretty well. I was now irritated with the lack of knowledge and concern my salespeople had about their performances.

I summarized, "So we don't know how many prospects there are or how frequently we are calling on them. Plus, we are losing existing customers to other suppliers because we can't fill their orders quickly enough. Does that about sum it up?"

Elaine rejoined the discussion. "If you're trying to blame us for your financial problems, I just don't agree," she said. "We're out every day working with customers. If the plant made quality buttons on time, we wouldn't be losing customers. When I bring a big order to

Larry he gives me a hundred excuses why his people can't meet the customer's requirements. You should be talking to the plant—not to us!" The meeting ended on time but it was clear there was no consensus regarding the problem or even that there was a problem.

"Well, that went well," I said to myself in my car on the way home. "I hope I have better luck with the plant managers and supervisors."

The plant management and I met in the cafeteria around ten the next morning. Attending the meeting were Larry (the plant manager), the materials manager, the quality control manager, and the two shift supervisors. Everyone seemed a little edgy because they rarely had attended this sort of meeting.

I began by explaining Superior Button's financial situation. The response was similar to the one I received from the salespeople. They shouldn't have to suffer due to low profits and the low profits were not their fault. I then presented the salespeople's concerns about poor order fulfillment and the CFO's concern about the high scrap rate.

Larry, the plant manager, spoke first. "There are two basic reasons we can't fill customer orders by the date they want them. First, the salespeople always wait till the last minute to give us the order. When they do, they don't fill out the orders accurately and we have to call the customer to find out what he really wants. Second, the quality of employee in the plant is much worse than it was when I started here 10 years ago. Even when we get a good employee, he doesn't stick around long. Our turnover is really high! It's no surprise we can't deliver on time and that we waste a lot of materials. We've all stayed on employees about this and even fired several who couldn't make the grade."

The finger-pointing was really getting on my nerves. The salespeople couldn't satisfy customers because the plant was slow. The plant was slow because the salespeople couldn't write up a proper order in advance of the request. No one was at fault and everyone was at fault.

I asked, "Why do we have such high turnover? We pay the plant people fair wages and provide a good benefits package."

Jenny, one of the shift supervisors, spoke up. "People we get now just don't want to work. They think they are owed a living. When we try to speed up production to meet deadlines we wind up with a lot of overtime. When we call them on the high scrap rate, they say that if they weren't so rushed they wouldn't make mistakes."

I really hate running a company, I thought. *I should have joined National Fasteners when they offered me a job five years ago.*

"What are you doing to solve these problems?" I pleaded.

"We have instituted some new policies and programs," Larry replied. "To hold down the payroll, we send everyone home when the work is finished for the day. Some of the workers have complained they can't make a good living when we do this—but if we don't need them, we don't need them. To cut down on the scrap rate, I have put in my own creation, the Keep Your Job Contest. Each Friday I post a ranking of each employee's pounds of scrap for the week. If someone remains at the top of the list for three consecutive weeks, we fire them."

I asked hesitantly, "Is the program working?"

Larry responded, "So far we've been able to target and fire six plant workers who produced excess scrap."

"But the scrap rate has increased over the past several months!" I exclaimed.

Larry responded, with some emotion, "We just haven't fired enough of the problem employees yet to see a big difference. But when the word gets out that you lose your job when you create too much scrap, I expect to see a big improvement!"

I was not too comforted by Larry's optimism. On the one hand, Larry said there was too much turnover. On the other hand, he is creating a work environment that causes turnover.

After the employee meetings, I was pessimistic about any

improvement in Superior Button's performance short of some unanticipated windfall. I knew that more of the same spelled financial disaster for Superior Button.

Chapter 8

Sid Visits First National Bank

I learned of First National Bank from my friend Susan whose brother worked there. She didn't tell me much, except to say that the way employees were managed and paid was radically different than conventional organizations. I was interested in better approaches to management, so I called Susan's brother.

"Hello. Jim Roberts speaking," he answered when I called.

"My name is Sid Murray," I said. "Your sister, Susan, said I should call you to find out more about how management works at First National."

There was a pause before Jim said, "Most people who visit us find what we do to be too radical and leave disappointed. I'd suggest it's probably not worth your time to visit."

Undaunted, I said, "I'm pretty open-minded and would very much like to see your operation, if it's not too much trouble."

"Okay" he said. "Can you come by Friday?"

"Sure," I said. "Will I be able to talk to some of your executives and managers?"

Jim responded, rather solemnly, "We don't have executives and managers at First National. The closest thing would be our planners and facilitators. I'm pretty sure some of them would spend a little time with you. See you Friday morning."

No executives and managers, only planners and facilitators? I guessed these were probably nothing more than new names for the same functions. Banks were notorious for renaming jobs but leaving the functions the same. Even so, I was very curious about First National and looked forward to my visit on Friday.

I arrived at First National at 9:00 a.m. Friday. The building was modern and around 10 stories tall. I parked, found the entrance, and walked in. The guard in the lobby called Jim who said he would be right down. As I was waiting, I was startled to see a small sign by the employee elevator that read, "No one may begin work before 8:00 a.m.—No exceptions." *Why did they need a sign like that?* I wondered.

Jim stepped off the elevator, looked around, and saw me seated near the guard desk. He smiled and walked over to me. "Hi, I'm Jim Roberts."

"Nice to meet you; Susan says you're a great guy! I'm Sid Murray. I really appreciate your taking the time to show me around." I followed Jim to the employee elevator (past the curious sign) and we moved up to the fifth floor. Jim ushered me into his office. On his door was a small plaque that read "Jim Roberts, performance system manager." *What was he—some computer guru or something?* I thought.

Jim pointed out a chair for me to sit in and then sat behind his desk. The office was rather Spartan for a high-level manager. Jim said, "What would you like to know about our company?"

I replied, "I guess I'd start by asking you what a performance system manager is and what sort of background you had that allowed you to become the bank's performance system manager."

"A performance system manager is responsible for the analysis, transition, integration, and results of an organization's performance system," Jim said offhandedly.

"What do you mean by a performance system?" I had no idea what Jim had just said.

"A performance system consists of all employee behaviors and results as they relate to selection, training, staffing, appraisal, management, promotion, compensation and work processes," Jim responded.

"Pretty much everything," I laughed. "So you are like a Human Resources Director."

"Not really," Jim said quickly. "The HR Department typically isn't judged by the success of the system. My job is to maximize employee performance and organizational profitability."

I thought I'd better understand Jim's job as he got into the details. So I decided to move on. "What sort of background do you have?"

Jim continued. "I came here with an MBA with a specialization in human resources. Given the owner's directives, however, I soon found out that I was not educated for the role I was to fill. I went back to college over several years and took additional courses in financial accounting, organizational psychology, applied behavior analysis, and industrial engineering."

"I see," I continued, "How many employees do you have?"

Jim said, "We have a total of 600 employees and 50 branches."

"Oh," I responded, "that doesn't seem like very many for a bank this size."

"It isn't," Jim replied matter-of-factly.

I asked, "How are you able to operate with such a lean staff?"

"All of our employees are cross-trained and our turnover is less than half a percent a year. Our management consists of only three planners and ten facilitators—plus me. We don't have any supervisors, branch managers, department managers or division managers."

"What?" I blurted out incredulously. "You're telling me that 14 people manage almost 600 employees?"

Jim smiled, "They don't manage employees in the conventional sense. Rather, they manage objectives, functions, and results."

"What do you mean?" I asked.

Jim said, "Our three planners are responsible for continuously researching the marketplace, our customer base, our competition, new technology, our stockholders, and general economic conditions. When any of these factors change, they make decisions about what we need to do to best adapt to any changes. They are our eyes and ears outside First National."

"I see," I said, "But who reports to them? Who implements their changes?"

"I do," Jim said proudly.

I was stunned. How in the world could Jim get around to 50 branches and 600 employees? *It must take years to get any changes implemented*, I thought. "Excuse me," I said in a strained voice. "Are you telling me that you, alone, provide all the management here? I find that impossible to believe!"

Jim answered, "It would be impossible in a traditional organization. Our founder purchased the bank 20 years ago. He retired from the bank five years ago—he was 55-years-old. In college, he had studied B.F. Skinner's behavior theory and his utopian novel, *Walden Two*. From this, he decided that conventional management hierarchies were an anachronism—given what we now know about behavior systems theory. One of his ideas was to cut out the middle man—to pay employees directly for measured results. Each employee is given a personal scorecard that lists the results and goals for the job. The measures are all objective—we eliminated the traditional annual performance review. When the planners wish to change the direction of all or part of the organization, they call me. I change the relevant employee scorecard measures or their priority weights to reflect the new direction."

Chapter 9

Sid Learns about
First National's Pay System

"But without managers and supervisors," I said, "How do you know if anyone ever gets anything done? Won't everyone just sit around and wait for their paychecks?"

"Not if they want to eat," Jim laughed. "None of our employees, including me, receive an hourly wage or a salary. We are paid on our personal and team results. The earnings for these results move up and down depending on bank profits for the month. If the bank does well, and I meet my goals, I earn a lot of money here. If the bank doesn't do well, or I don't perform well, I could receive no pay for the month—but that's never happened, knock on wood!"

"You're telling me that everyone here is on a sort of piece-rate or straight-commission pay plan?" I asked—in a higher pitched voice than I meant to have.

"That's right," Jim replied.

"That can't possibly work!" I said, getting really agitated by his smug confidence. "First-off, you have to pay minimum wage and overtime."

Jim responded, "We do have to track timesheet hours to conform to the wage and hour laws. However, it's not really an issue since all of our hourly workers earn well over minimum wage anyway."

Jim continued, "Let me ask you a question. Does our country's economy work well most of the time?"

"Compared to other countries and past economies, I would have to say yes," I answered.

"Would you say our free-enterprise system produces more goods, services, and wealth for its citizens than other systems, for example socialism?"

The question seemed rhetorical, but I said *yes* anyway.

Jim sat back in his chair and looked at the ceiling. I could tell I was in for a lengthy lecture. "My question to you is, who manages this complicated system of exchanges?" he asked.

I thought a minute. Who *did* manage the system? In the old Soviet Union, they had a bureaucracy that decided what would be grown, by whom, and when. They also decided how it would be distributed and what the prices would be. But, in a true, free-enterprise system, there is no managing bureaucracy. How do things get done? Then I recalled something from my college economics course, something Adam Smith called *The Invisible Hand.*

In Smith's view, complex interactions were directed by each party's self-interest. First National's employees were really self-employed. Their customer was the organization. Their products and services were the specified scorecard results. First National was a market within a market. The desired goods and services were determined by the planners based on demands from the external marketplace. These outcomes were then defined for the employees on their performance scorecards. The planner was a vendor to the end customer. The employee was a vendor to the planner.

In thinking all this through, I saw a critical flaw. "If First National fails to make a profit, then no one would be paid!" I said. "I would imagine everyone would bail out the first time profits declined."

Jim explained, "If our profits decline we can either lay off employees or let them leave on their own. The ones that stay are those that believe they can help turn the business around and believe they will make up for current lost pay by sharing in future success."

"So, there has to be a lot of trust and openness between labor, management, and ownership," I concluded.

"You're right—that's absolutely essential," Jim agreed. "But, in the longer view, the employee is better paid and more secure in our system."

"Really?" I said skeptically.

"Really!" Jim responded. "In the traditional wage-and-salary system when the company profits increase the gain often doesn't translate to salary increases for the employees."

"Yeah, that's because owners are greedy," I said.

Jim replied, "Well, sometimes that's true, but there is a much deeper economic issue. Over the years, wages and salaries have come to be viewed by employees as entitlements. They believe they are owed their pay regardless of the financial status of the company or the company's ability to pay. Salaries only go up—never down, even when profits decline. Consequently, companies are very reluctant to increase pay because it has become a guaranteed, fixed expense."

"So," I said, "The employee doesn't get an increased salary when profits increase because it has become a guarantee?"

"Right," Jim said, "But the current wage-and-salary system causes more problems for employees than that. When profits decline, employees expect salaries to remain the same. This sounds like a good deal for employees until you dig a little deeper. What typically happens to employees when a company experiences bad financial times for an extended period?" Jim asked.

"They get laid off!" I exclaimed. "The employee loses out both in good times and bad times the more I think about it."

"Right again," Jim agreed. "Basically, there is no free lunch. In our system, when times get tough, everyone takes a pay cut rather than some employees losing their jobs."

Jim went on. "The wage-and-salary system was introduced on a large scale in Henry Ford's plants in the early twentieth century. Before then, many manufacturing employees were paid a piece rate, both here and in Europe. If you look back to the nineteenth century, most of us were farmers. If we farmed well, we did well. If we didn't, we didn't do so well. After World War II, there was also high inflation which spawned the idea of automatic annual increases in pay."

"So our wage-and-salary system is only a hundred or so years old?" I asked.

"That's basically true," Jim responded.

"That's very interesting," I said. "If it makes such good sense to pay for performance, then why aren't all companies converting to your approach?"

Jim laughed, too long, I thought. "There are many more issues in pay for performance than just money," he said.

"Like what?" I asked. "It seems simple enough to me. The more someone does, the more she gets."

"Does what?" Jim responded.

"Does whatever they are supposed to do," I replied defensively.

Jim said, "Yes, but how do you know what they have done?"

"You could ask the supervisor," I ventured.

"You mean something like an annual performance review?" Jim asked.

I could sense Jim was setting me up. I knew from my own work history, and running my own company, that the annual review was a notoriously invalid measure of employee performance.

Jim began, "Another *innovation* of the wage-and-salary system is that we stopped measuring actual performance. This happened because pay was severed from performance. To pay employees a wage or salary you only have to keep up with the hours they worked—not whether they accomplished anything!

"For example, I was visiting with the human resources director at another company a few years ago. The payroll supervisor interrupted our meeting. She was obviously quite distressed. I asked her what was wrong. She blushed, and informed me that they had been sending a paycheck to an employee who was dead. The employee had died several months earlier, but no one told payroll. I'm sure you'd agree that a system that pays dead people is not performance based!" Jim smirked.

"Well, I can see how that might happen, but still employee performance is evaluated at least once a year by the supervisor," I argued.

"Is it?" Jim questioned.

"Sure," I said. "I suppose some companies do a better job than others with their annual review process. But most companies do have annual performance reviews."

"Let's talk about annual reviews," Jim seemed to light up. "We are asking a supervisor to mentally average 250 work days and come up with an overall assessment of performance. If I asked you how often you felt ill, depressed, or happy last year, how would you answer?"

"Well, I guess that would be difficult to answer accurately," I said. "But I have a general notion of how I felt last year."

"Did you keep a log?" Jim chuckled. "Are you sure your opinion isn't colored by recent events or exceptionally bad or good days during the year?"

"Well maybe," I admitted, "but those are subjective experiences. The supervisor is asked to evaluate real results."

"No he isn't," Jim proclaimed, "He's asked for his impressions of an employee's results. Usually, no actual data are collected. Let me give you an example. Before I joined the bank I was a performance improvement consultant. One of my first jobs was to improve wine sales for a restaurant chain. Wine had a high profit margin, but their sales were way below those of their competitors. The first thing I did at the pilot restaurant was to ask the general manager and the two shift managers to individually rank the sales performances of the seven cocktail waitresses. They all agreed on who was best and who was worst, but had some disagreement about their middle rankings. After some discussion, we had complete agreement on the rankings.

"I then did something radical. I retrieved their point-of-sales data for the past several months and organized it by each cocktail waitress's actual sales. The result was really shocking. The best sales person, according to the data, was the cocktail waitress the managers rated as the worst. The one they rated best was actually average. How could they have been so wrong, especially in a restaurant where they could directly observe the waitresses' performances?"

I thought this over. "Maybe they weren't just rating them on performance," I guessed.

"Exactly!" Jim exclaimed. "What do you think they were really rating them on?"

"Well, I suppose how much they liked them?" I said cautiously.

"You bet," Jim agreed. "I observed that the waitress they rated as the worst did not get along well with the managers—but did with customers. She must have had some sort of problem with authority. In fact, because I wore a suit, and spent time with the managers, she saw me as part of management and was surly to me as well. Given this, I'm sure I would have rated her low also. Let me ask you something. With your management experience, do you find that high performers are more independent and more often challenge manager decisions and authority?"

"No question," I said thinking of Elaine. "My top salesperson can be a real pain in the neck!"

Jim responded, "So why don't you fire him?"

I laughed, "He is a she and I can't afford to."

"And why is that?" Jim asked.

"Because she accounts for over half of my sales," I said.

"But what if you didn't know that?" Jim queried.

"I suppose if I didn't know what she actually contributed to my company, I would have fired her a long time ago," I realized.

"The cocktail waitress ratings were also wrong for other reasons," Jim continued. "Remember, we had three men rating seven women. Do you see a potential problem?" Jim looked directly at me.

"Well, I suppose they would rate the ones they liked best higher. It could also have been a beauty contest," I said.

Jim responded, "Exactly. And I found this same situation in 30 other restaurants. The women who were pretty and socialized with the managers almost always received higher rankings. Do you see anything wrong with that?" he asked.

"Sure, the restaurant's not a cocktail party; it's a business!" I declared.

"So we agree that objective measurement is much superior to subjective impressions?" Jim asked.

"Yeah, but it would be a lot of trouble to measure what each employee actually did," I said. "It doesn't seem necessary, anyway. Without objective measures people come to work and perform pretty well. The wage-and-salary system seems to do all right as far as I can see," I said guardedly.

Jim leaned back in his chair. "And that brings us to the nub of the real issue. Let's get a cup of coffee and we'll get into it."

Jim and I walked down the hall past a number of cubicles. I noticed that everyone seemed to be working, but relaxed. When we entered the kitchen, I was surprised to find three employees playing cards at one of the tables. I expected a reaction from Jim, but there was none. Walking back to Jim's office, I asked him, "Aren't you concerned that those employees were playing cards in the middle of the day?"

"Why should I be?" Jim asked. "They don't have anything to do until the checks and deposits arrive from the branches. A lot of them go shopping or go home until the next batch of work arrives."

"What!" I exclaimed. "That seems really inefficient! You are paying people to play cards or go shopping!"

Jim sighed. "No, we are paying them to process checks and deposits. If there aren't any items to process, we don't pay them," he said. "If they get more efficient, they can either find other things to do, and earn more money, or take time off. I assume they are playing cards because the next batch will arrive soon. You are still mired in pay-for-time logic. We don't pay for time—we pay for results!"

I immediately saw the error in my thinking. These employees weren't paid by the hour but by how much they produced. If there was nothing to do, they could either find other work or take time off. *What a sensible approach*, I thought, admiringly.

We sat back down in Jim's office. "You were talking about how much trouble it would be to measure employee results rather than simply pay them for their time," Jim began. "There are a lot of critics of what we do here. They argue that good employees are self-motivated and work because they are responsible people. This is a naïve view of things, at best. If people are self-motivated we shouldn't have to pay them at all! What would happen at your business if you quit paying people altogether and simply relied on their self-motivation to get the job done?"

"They'd quit," I replied.

"Right," Jim said. "The critics are confusing work with play. Of course no one has to pay me to watch television or go fishing. These are activities that are naturally reinforcing to me. But processing checks and deposits is work. We have never had a clerk purchase a data-entry machine and process items at home for fun," Jim said chuckling. "People work to earn a living."

"Okay, so much for self-motivation," I said. "That view never made much sense to me anyway. But you haven't really answered my question. Employees do get an incentive for working now. It's called a paycheck. Why should I want to go to the trouble to measure what they do?"

"You have asked the big question," Jim said solemnly. "Let me give you a quick behavior-theory lesson. There are basically two ways to get someone to do something they aren't naturally interested in. We can either reward them or threaten them. There is no third option. Here at First National we have chosen the first approach. Most other organizations have chosen the second."

"What? You're kidding?" I said, startled by Jim's assertion.

"No I'm not," Jim, retorted. "Employees don't work to get a paycheck, the paycheck is automatic. What's really going on is that they come to work to avoid losing the check or facing supervisor and peer criticism. This is termed *negative reinforcement*. A positive reinforcement arrangement says, 'If you do this, you will get this.' A salary really says, 'If you don't do this, you won't get this.'"

I found all this very confusing and Jim could tell I was perplexed.

He continued, "I once was hired to teach prison guards how to manage prisoners using positive reinforcement. The guards quickly became bored with my lectures so I decided an animal demonstration would liven things up.

"I brought two Skinner boxes to the classroom with two white rats. The Skinner box is used in many animal behavioral research programs. It is a Plexiglas box about one-foot high, wide, and deep. I would demonstrate the concepts of positive and negative reinforcement with these boxes and two rats. In the positive reinforcement box was a lever on the wall that was connected to a food dispenser. If the rat pressed the lever, food was dispensed. I could have simply waited until the rat accidentally pressed the lever, but this would have taken a long time.

"Instead, I used a technique termed *shaping* to speed up the process. In shaping, the experimenter delivers food to the rat for 'successive approximations' to the desired, lever-pressing behavior. If the rat faces the lever, he is reinforced; then reinforced again, if he approaches, then if he touches the lever, and so on. A good shaper can teach a rat to press the lever in 15 minutes or so. I wasn't so good, and it took over 30 minutes to get the rat to press the lever. After that of course, the rat pressed the lever on his own, with no further intervention from me.

"Now I was ready to demonstrate negative reinforcement in the second box with the other rat. This box had an electric shock grid in the bottom and no food dispenser. I could apply shock to the rat's paws. When I turned the shock on, the rat jumped and happened to jump on the lever that then turned the shock off. He quickly learned to keep pressing the lever to keep the shock from coming back on. The rat was pressing the lever in a matter of minutes.

"I then asked the guards for their comments on these two procedures. One guard spoke up immediately saying that the negative reinforcement worked much faster and I didn't have to feed the rat. Everyone else nodded in agreement. The consensus was that negative reinforcement was faster and cheaper. I was depressed. My demonstration had backfired. I decided to give the guards a 10-minute break while I collected my thoughts."

Jim continued, "One of the guards went over to the chambers and picked up the rat in the positive reinforcement chamber to play with it. When another guard saw this, he tried to pick up the rat in the negative reinforcement chamber. The rat struggled and then bit the guard who screamed in pain and had a lot of trouble extricating the rat from his finger. After everything settled back down, I asked the guards, "Now, what do think of positive vs. negative reinforcement?" I said triumphantly.

One guard replied, "Well, negative reinforcement works, but you just don't want to be around the rat."

I continued, "When you go to get these two rats from their home cages in the morning, how do you expect the positively reinforced rat will greet you?"

Almost in unison, the guards said, "He'll be anxious to see you because he gets fed in the chamber."

"Right," I replied. "In fact, they act much like your pet dog or cat, who is waiting for you when you bring their food to them. And how will you be greeted by the negatively reinforced rat?"

Again, almost in unison, the guards responded, "The rat will be afraid of you and won't want to go."

"Right again," I said. "They move to the back of the cage and grab onto the wire bottom of the cage. You have to wear protective gloves and pull them out of the cage. When you finally get them to the chamber, they often spread-eagle to keep from being placed in the cage. When you finally get them in the cage, they immediately go over and begin pressing the lever to keep from getting shocked."

Jim finished his example and asked me, "Does the negatively reinforced rat remind you of employees in any way?"

"Yes, many employees complain and argue and don't want to come to work, come late, take long breaks, and leave early. Is this why?" I asked.

"Often so; of course other issues also come into play," Jim replied.

"Almost all animal trainers now use positive reinforcement to teach animals. Can you imagine Sea World trainers trying to use negative reinforcement with Shamu the killer whale? Unfortunately, most employees are still managed through negative reinforcement. Many of our managers are not as enlightened as animal trainers."

"So, what you are saying is that you have to measure employee results to use positive reinforcement?" I asked.

"Exactly!" Jim seemed impressed with my quick understanding of the implications. "You can only positively reinforce measured results. If you choose not to measure results, you must resort to manager perceptions and negative reinforcement to manage employees. The consequences of this decision are profound. The pervasive use of negative reinforcement has many serious downsides for organizations. As we just discussed, absenteeism and low morale are results. Also, employees only perform to minimum expectations, are placed in an adversarial relationship with managers, and employee initiative and innovation suffers."

"Wait a minute," I said. "Why do employee initiative and innovation suffer?"

"This is possibly one of the most devastating effects of negative reinforcement on an organization's success," Jim said. "I don't want to bore you with too many anecdotes, but I can best explain what we are talking about with one more, if I may."

"Please do," I said.

Jim began, "I was speaking at a quality conference a few years ago. I was discussing these issues with one of the other speakers on the dais who happened to be from Japan. He gave me this example of the adverse impact of negative reinforcement on initiative and innovation. When an emperor ruled Japan, the emperor had 99 rules of conduct for his subjects. He had his Samurai warriors enforce these rules. If someone broke a rule, the warriors would drag the person out of their home, take them to the town square, and cut their head off with a large sword.

"But what made the system so effective for so long was that the emperor never published the 99 rules! You can imagine the impact of this combination on his subjects' initiative and innovation. They were probably afraid to even take a different route home from work in the afternoon."

"Sounds pretty frightening," I agreed. "So what you are saying is that when fear is used to manage people, they tend to be reactive and offer few original ideas."

"*Don't volunteer and don't rock the boat* is the motto of the negatively reinforced," Jim agreed.

Jim got out of his chair and said, "Let's take a break so I can make some phone calls. We'll meet next with Ellen, one of our facilitators, at two o'clock on the fifth floor, room 505. See you there."

Sid Meets a Facilitator

I arrived at Ellen's office before Jim. I knocked on the door and was greeted by a tall, serious-looking woman whose initial demeanor was soon contradicted by her wide smile.

Ellen said, "You must be Sid? Jim said you were coming. He told me you own your company and wanted to know more about our performance system approach to management. Have a seat over there," she said as she pointed to a chair in the corner of the room.

I looked around the room and found it was wallpapered with hundreds of small graphs. They appeared to be arranged by areas of the bank. Each graph had handwritten notes all over it.

"Would you like something to drink?" Ellen asked.

"No thank you, I'm fine," I said. "While we're waiting for Jim, would you mind telling me how you became a facilitator here at the bank?"

She laughed and said, "Probably because I was the most argumentative and resistant manager when the new system was first proposed."

"Really? Why?" I asked, anticipating her answer from my earlier discussion with Jim.

Ellen responded, "I was very career-oriented when I arrived at the bank. I had a master's degree from Stanford and worked at a bank as a teller and then a loan officer during my schooling. I attended the graduate banking school after that. My personal goal was to make executive vice president of lending before I was 30. I could have too, had they not introduced the new system."

"I guess you were pretty disappointed," I commiserated.

"I wasn't just disappointed; I was furious," Ellen said. I could see the anger returning as she thought about it. "I had put all this effort into my career ladder and then they eliminated all the rungs. When my Dad asked me what I was doing at the bank, I almost choked telling him I was a facilitator. I wasn't even an executive facilitator, just a plain old, run-of-the-mill facilitator."

"You lost all the prestige that goes with the title of executive vice president," I said.

"Right, I almost began looking for another job immediately," Ellen said, "But I decided to wait a while and see what the new system was all about. After all, the bank I worked at before was always announcing some program du jour and it never amounted to anything. I figured that this would probably fade away also."

Ellen continued, "I met with our president, Terry, about a week after the announcement. I trusted Terry and respected him, even though many of the managers thought he was somewhat of a dreamer. I told Terry how upset I was with his eliminating my career path and how hard I had worked to achieve my goals. Terry listened closely and then said something I will never forget. He said, 'I understand what you want to *be*, but what do you want to *do*?' I asked, 'What do you mean?'

Ellen replied, "Terry told me, 'Being an executive vice president gives you a lot of status. It's a great thing to tell your folks and impress your friends. It also means you have control over many people who will try to ingratiate themselves to you. It comes with a big office, good pay, and other perks. Are these things your goal?'

"I said to Terry, 'You're putting a bad face on it but of course it's what I want. What else is there?'

"Terry responded, 'What if I gave you the title and all those things, but your job would be to sit in your big office and study proposed legislation that might affect the bank?'

"I said, 'That doesn't interest me at all. It sounds really boring,' and I was frightened that Terry might be serious.

"Terry asked me again, 'Then what is it that you want to do? Imagine the perfect job. Tell me what your day would be like.'

"I reflected on this for several minutes and said, 'Well, I guess I like working with other people and solving problems. I've always been good with people and enjoy helping them overcome obstacles. I was the editor of my high school yearbook and in college I organized our guest speaker series. I've always had a knack for getting things done.'

"Terry said, 'So what you like to do is work with other people and solve problems?'

"I told him, 'In a nutshell, that's it!' I then realized, I had never really given this much thought.

"Terry asked, 'Do you think that the traditional executive vice president of lending job lets you do those things?'

"I replied, 'Sure!'

"Terry then asked me, 'What if I told you that in the traditional EVP role your people would often tell you what you want to hear and make excuses for failures rather than try to solve problems? That people would generally be more interested in impressing you than finding opportunities to improve the organization? That much of your day would be involved in listening to complaints, demands, and gossip? That in turn you would do the same with me? And, the rest of your day would be spent sitting in all kinds of committee meetings?'

"I replied, 'I'm sure you're exaggerating. Maybe some managers create that kind of situation but I wouldn't.'

"Terry said dramatically, 'It's not you creating the situation, it *is* the situation! Who would decide whether one of your subordinates receives a raise or promotion?'

I said that I would decide and he asked me if I would make these decisions based on my opinion of my subordinates' abilities.

"I said, 'Of course!'"

The rest of the conversation between Ellen and Terry went as follows:

"The key word, here, is *opinion*," Terry said. "You would make the decisions based upon your opinion. So, does the smart subordinate focus on improving your opinion of him?"

"Well, yes," Ellen said hesitantly.

"In the same vein, would you focus on improving my opinion of you?" Terry asked.

"Yes, again," Ellen responded. "Okay, I get it. We're all trying to impress each other rather than working together to improve the organization's success. That's your point, isn't it?"

"Right!" Terry agreed.

Terry sat back in his chair. He said, "When I decided to go into business for myself, one of my main reasons was to get out from under a boss I didn't like and I wasn't good at corporate politics. I became a bank consultant and was self-employed. No more boss! Was I right?"

Ellen thought about this for a minute. *Was he right?* It sounded good—no boss to impress or tell you what to do. But something was wrong. Ellen had friends who tried working for themselves. Some were successful, but many weren't. What was the difference?

"Something is wrong with your idea of no boss, but I'm not sure what it is," she finally said.

Terry said, "There *is* a boss—it's your customer! The self-employed must impress his customers in the same way the corporate employee must impress his boss. If you do, you will get additional business and a good reference. If you don't, you'll get fired."

Terry continued, "Let me ask you this. Which organization will be more successful, the one in which everyone is trying to impress each other, or the one in which everyone is trying to impress customers?"

"That's easy," Ellen said. "The one that is customer-focused is going to be more successful than the one that is only focused inwardly."

"If that's true, then doesn't it make sense that we get rid of the internal management hierarchy that disconnects employees from customers?" Terry asked.

"In theory," Ellen said unconvincingly.

"You don't seem to agree yet," Terry said. "Let me give you a couple of examples of how banks disconnect their employees from their customers. Our tellers are our front-line contact people for our depositors. In the traditional bank, the teller position is an entry-level job that pays a modest hourly wage. The wage is based on how many hours the teller works, not how many customers she serves. On the other hand, if the teller irritates a customer or fails to balance her drawer at the end of the day, she will be reprimanded, suspended, or even fired. Given these things, when a customer walks in the branch lobby do you think tellers are glad to see them?"

Ellen saw where he was going. "No, I guess in that situation they would see customers as a risk rather than an opportunity. Each customer only represents a chance to get fired."

"Exactly," Terry agreed. "Through paying for time and punishing errors, the bank has unknowingly put the teller and the customer in an adversarial relationship. Why don't you apply this analysis to the customer service representative who opens new accounts for customers in the branch? The bank's business goal is to get the customer to open several accounts and purchase various services. How does pay for time and management by exception affect this goal?"

"Let's see," Ellen said. "Just like the teller, the CSR is paid an hourly wage. If the CSR convinces the customer to open additional accounts or purchase additional services, then he has to complete the paperwork. This will take more time, which would cause other customers to have to wait and they might get irritated. Further, the chance of a mistake increases with each new additional account or service. The best strategy for the CSR is to serve as few customers as possible and to open the minimum number of accounts for each customer— the opposite of the bank's business objective!"

"Now let's try one closer to home—the loan officer," Terry suggested.

"Well," Ellen said. "It's still the case that the more customers they serve, the more opportunity there is for documentation errors or, worse, making loans that default. It's also true that if they see a lot of prospects there will be a higher number of rejected loans and therefore more complaints. But there is one key difference. Banks track loan officer sales and set sales goals for their officers."

"Right! And what happens if they fail to meet the goals?" Terry asked.

"Usually they are asked to justify why they didn't make goal," Ellen responded. "We all got pretty good at these justifications over time. The bank's rates were too high. The bank didn't offer the right kinds of loans. The bank didn't advertise enough. No one was interested in getting a loan. No one we saw was eligible. We didn't have good or up-to-date prospect lists. We didn't have time to find prospects because of excessive paperwork, and so on."

"Now let's get back to the issue of the difference between self-employment and working in a corporation," Terry said. "If you were lending people your own money how would things be different?"

Now Ellen saw where Terry was headed. The more loans she booked, the more money she would make. If she made bad loans, she would lose money.

"How much time would you spend dreaming up excuses for why you weren't selling?" Terry asked.

"There wouldn't be any point to it," she said. "I'm working for myself."

"Someone once said that entrepreneurs create organizations that they would never work in," Terry said. "Do you see what they meant?"

"Yeah," Ellen said. "The entrepreneur deals with customers. If he is successful, he directly benefits. No one is trying to scare him into working. But when his business grows he creates an organization based on internal politics and fear—the very things he, himself, escaped from."

Terry said, "What I am trying to do here at the bank is to create an organization in which everyone is self-employed. One step is this venture is to eliminate the traditional management hierarchy and its politics and intimidation. Everyone becomes a partner and stakeholder in the bank and personally shares in the financial benefits of our success. Is this a vision you can buy in to?" he asked.

"Possibly," Ellen said. "I see how the management hierarchy gets in the way of customer service and employee initiative. I agree we'd be better off without it. I can also see that as a true partner in the bank my earnings could actually exceed what I would have earned as a traditional executive vice president. However, you haven't explained what my new role, as a facilitator would be. Does the role meet my interests in working with people and solving problems?"

"That *is* the role," Terry said bluntly. "Instead of supervising and judging the lending people, as the facilitator your job will be to help them maximize their performances and personal earnings. Employees will seek you out to help them solve problems and create opportunities, since you will no longer be their judge. The better they perform, and the more they earn, the better you have performed as a facilitator and the more you will earn. By the way, your earnings in our new system are unlimited if you place 100 percent of your pay at risk, just as they would be if you were self-employed. Of course this unlimited opportunity is a two-edged sword. If the bank doesn't perform well, you would earn less than your old EVP salary."

"I'm not worried about my performance," Ellen said defensively. "If people want my help, and I have the authority and tools to give them the help, then I know I will succeed."

"Good, I knew you'd say that," Terry said with obvious admiration. "You will have total authority to make changes in the lending division. You will also have the resources and tools you need. Our new planners will provide you detailed market analyses to help you plan your sales and service strategies. They will also continually review changes in consumer demands, new technology, new competition, and economic conditions to assist you."

"You mean I'll actually be given the information directly rather than simply told what to do?" Ellen asked suspiciously.

"Exactly—the lending division is your business," Terry said.

"That sounds great," Ellen said. "We should have done this long ago instead of keeping the information at the top and filtering it down through the old chain of command. I never understood why information was withheld in the first place." *Then it hit her. Information is power. In the old hierarchical system people maintained their power by holding back information. In the new system, there was no need to do this.*

"Okay, I'm in," she said. "But if my pay is based on how well the employees perform that I assist, I need a good deal of training in performance analysis and improvement. These weren't covered in college or the graduate banking school."

"All six of our new facilitators will receive intensive training in behavior analysis and performance improvement," Terry promised.

When Ellen had ended her story, she looked over at me. I could see she was embarrassed that she had gone on so long about her meeting with the bank president. She said, "Sorry for such a long answer to your short question. Anyway, that's why I decided to become a facilitator at the bank."

"Any regrets?" I asked.

Ellen replied, "Only that I wasted several years working my way up in the old system. I really find the facilitator role challenging and satisfying. My need for prestige has been fulfilled by the honest gratitude I receive from those I help. Further, my pay is now tied directly to bottom-line performance rather than petty politics. And, yes, my earnings are typically much greater than the EVP salary I gave up. Unfortunately, some of the executive managers turned out to be ineffective facilitators even with the training. Eventually their earnings were so low they left the bank and were replaced by people we recruited from inside and outside the bank."

"Would you tell me about the training you received?" I asked. Just then Jim, the performance system manager, walked into Ellen's office.

"Hi, guys," he said cheerfully.

Ellen replied, "Ah, the Wizard of Oz arrives at last."

"Thanks Dorothy," he said matter-of-factly. "Any wicked witches today?"

"Always," Ellen said. "I was about to explain to Sid how we facilitators do our work. Do you want to sit in?"

"Wouldn't miss it," said Jim, sitting down in the other chair.

Ellen walked over to the far wall in her office where a large diagram hung. "I can best explain this using our constraint diagnostic," Ellen announced. "Employee performance constraints can be categorized into three broad categories: the opportunity to perform, the capability, and the job context. We know that 99 percent of the time performance is being held back due to one or more of these."

"How do you know which one is the constraint?" I asked. I was very pleased to see how systematic the facilitator role appeared to be.

Ellen explained. "There are basically three methods for determining which category is the likely source of the performance constraint. These methods are trend analysis, direct observation, and interviews.

"In trend analysis you look at a graph of the target performance to determine its trend and variability. For example, if the same employees have remained in the job, but the trend is highly variable or declining, the constraint is probably not capability. Another example would be a department that rarely completes all the work due. This situation is certainly not a work opportunity problem.

"Sometimes I can't tell from the performance charts what the constraint category is. In that case I spend some time in the department interviewing employees and directly observing the area. I can usually figure out what the constraint is in a few days."

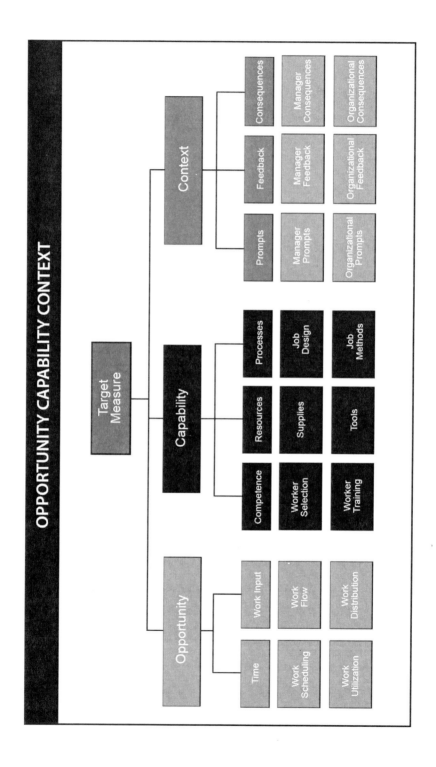

"Why don't the managers or workers do this themselves?" I asked. "Oops, I forgot there are no managers, are there?"

Jim chimed in, "No managers in the traditional sense of supervision and evaluation. However, the employees in an area do agree on a team coordinator to whom they pay a small override from their earnings for scheduling and interdepartmental coordination."

"Anyway," Ellen said, somewhat annoyed at the interruption, "the employees in the area do not have the training or third-party perspective we facilitators have. Further, only I can authorize solutions that require significant expenditures, process improvements, or staffing changes.

"Let me give you an example of the process," Ellen said. "What job are you having problems with at your company?"

"Salespeople!" I exclaimed.

Ellen replied, "What specific performance result is a problem?"

"Easy, some of them don't sell enough," I said as I anxiously waited for her analysis.

Ellen asked, "Are sales consistently low, highly variable, or declining over time?"

"In my opinion," I said, "They are consistently low. "I base this on a comparison with my competitors' sales."

"Okay," Ellen replied." When performance is consistently low it can be due to any of the constraint categories: opportunity, capability, or context. One way to determine if opportunity is the problem is to see whether any of your salespeople are meeting your goals. If a few are, than the opportunity must be there and you more likely have a capability or context issue. Do you have a few people that are performing at goal?"

"Not really!" I answered. "Oh, they may hit the goal now and then, but never consistently."

"If no one is performing well, then it may be the job context. Do your salespeople know whom to sell to, what, when, where, and how?" Ellen asked.

"They have all been through the same training our competitors give their salespeople," I replied.

Ellen asked, "Do they know they are not performing at goal?"

"We have weekly sales meetings and go over each person's sales the previous week and what the goals are," I said, now somewhat smugly.

"Is there a personal benefit to them for selling?" Ellen asked.

"They earn a 5 percent commission on each sale," I said. I was beginning to think Ellen was not going to figure out the problem after all.

"So the constraint is likely in the opportunity-to-perform category," Ellen said confidently. "There are two major issues in this category: poor quality or delayed work input and insufficient time. Do you provide your salespeople with up-to-date lists of qualified prospects?"

"I'm pretty sure we do," I said hesitantly. "Generally, we expect them to develop their own leads."

"I see," Ellen said. "And what is the procedure they use for finding prospects?"

"They are supposed to be professional salespeople and know how to develop leads on their own," I stated, somewhat embarrassed by my answer.

"Sounds like we need to investigate how leads are generated and distributed. Then we could develop a more systematic method. No prospects, no new sales!" Ellen said triumphantly.

I knew she was right. "I guess I've been blaming the salespeople instead of identifying and solving the problem."

Jim spoke up, "The blame game is a national pastime. If only parents had good children; if only doctors had good patients; if only actors had good audiences; if only managers had good employees. The blame game is played often in organizations where excuses for failure are required, and no one knows how to analyze and solve the real underlying problems."

Jim said to Ellen, "Thanks for your time. We really appreciate it. I promised Sid I would let him meet one of our planners this afternoon, so we need to get going."

"Hope I was helpful to you," Ellen said.

"It was a pleasure to meet you," I replied. "I really appreciate the time you gave me and your candor."

As we walked down the hall, Jim asked me if I would like to get a cup of coffee in the break room before we met the planner. I agreed and we walked to the break room. As I poured my coffee, I noticed a small group of people meeting at a large, circular table in a corner of the room. The group was looking at a chart similar to the ones I saw earlier in Jim's office. The discussion was quite animated.

I asked Jim, "Who are those people over there?"

He responded, "They are the information technology team. They are meeting to discuss the results of one of their performance improvement projects or PIPs. I happen to know the target measure for the discussion is computer network up time. The woman leading the discussion is their coordinator. The man sitting next to her is their division facilitator."

"Do you think they'd mind if we listened in while we drink our coffee?" I asked.

"I'll go over and ask them," Jim said. He walked over to the group and talked to them briefly. "No problem," he said when he came back. "All they wanted to know was whether or not you were from a competitor bank."

I introduced myself and Jim pulled some chairs up near the group. The coordinator, Jill, continued talking. "You can see from this trend chart that up time has improved 25 percent over the past three months. Our improvement plan was a major success. You guys had a great idea in reassigning the routers. However, we've still got a ways to go to hit our up-time goal of 99.8 percent. Any more ideas?"

A young man spoke up. He looked to be in his early twenties. "We can't find any economically feasible way to protect the network from major storm surges. But, I've been thinking, maybe we could reduce the time it takes to reboot the network?"

The facilitator entered into the discussion. "Would you say the constraint on rapid rebooting is an opportunity, capability, or context problem?"

Everyone in the group seemed to know what he was asking. An older man, Steve, said, "It's clearly a poor quality input problem. We get bad electricity!" Several people laughed and then he said, "Seriously, I believe it may be a context constraint—specifically a feedback problem."

The facilitator asked, "What kind of feedback problem?"

Steve replied, "When the system goes down no one is specifically assigned to bring it back up. The result is a delay until someone decides to begin the reboot process."

"I see," said the facilitator. "You're not so much talking about feedback as you are prompting. Are there no clear assignments as to who is to reboot the system?" Everyone in the group shook their heads no.

"What about written reboot procedures?" he asked. Again, everyone shook their heads no.

"I think we're on to something," he said.

Chapter 11

Sid Meets a Planner

It was time to visit the planner so Jim and I excused ourselves from the meeting and headed toward the planner's office. When we arrived, a surprisingly young man, who appeared to be in his thirties, greeted us. "Hi, I'm Edward Timmons," he announced.

Jim said, "Thanks for letting us visit. This is Sid Murray."

Edward said, "Nice to meet you, Sid. Come on in."

Entering Edward's office was an initial shock. Instead of an executive suite, the office looked more like a stock trader's office or a military war room. There were computers everywhere sandwiched in between ceiling-high shelves of notebooks and periodicals. Then I remembered. The planners were not traditional executives any more than the facilitators were traditional managers. As I thought this through, the appearance of the office began to make more sense.

"Who have you met so far?" Edward asked.

I responded, "Well, I've talked with Jim here, and one of your facilitators, Ellen. Oh, and I briefly sat in on a team meeting with the IT group."

"So you're getting a pretty good idea how our performance system concept works?" Edward asked.

"I think so," I said. "Everyone has been very willing to share information and take some time with me."

"We're quite proud of our system," Edward smiled. "I firmly believe we are 20-to-50 years ahead of other organizations in the way we conduct business."

"Everything is certainly different," I agreed. "I'm really interested in learning about your planner role."

"Did Jim explain that there are three planners here?" Edward asked.

"Yes, are each of you assigned to a division?" I inquired.

"No, we are each assigned a functional area. I plan for consumer demand and regulatory changes, Juanita is our technology planner, and Tim plans for competition and changes in the economy. We meet weekly to compare notes and prepare our strategies and tactics."

"So you prepare an annual strategic plan for the bank?" I asked.

"Not really," Edward said simply. "We don't think in years, or really any kind of set time frame. We react to events. New regulations, change in consumer demands, new technology, competitor changes, changes in the economy, and so on are what drive our planning. We like to think we can forecast some of these changes and react in advance, but often things change too quickly or in ways we don't anticipate."

"I see," I said. "Once you decide on a strategic change, how do you communicate the strategy and get the employees to shift their priorities. I've found this really difficult in my organization. We have meetings but many people don't attend, understand, agree, or change. It must be especially difficult here with no management hierarchy to relay the message to the troops."

Edward glanced knowingly at Jim. Jim looked over at me and said, "Remember the scorecards we talked about this morning?" he asked.

"Yes," I said.

Jim continued, "When Edward and the other planners arrive at a new strategy, they call me in. We review the scorecard measures as they relate to the new strategy. Sometimes we just change the priority weights of the relevant measures on the scorecards. Other times we have to change the performance goals. In some cases we have to add or remove measures from scorecards. And finally, we may have to link a measure to scorecards that don't currently have it to get participation from new target groups of employees."

I asked, "You mean you do all your communicating with employees through the scorecards?"

"Let me ask you something," Jim responded. "How do customers ultimately communicate with their vendors regarding what they want, how quickly, at what quality, and at what price?"

I thought about this for a minute and said, "I guess they choose to buy or not to buy from the vendor," I said.

"Exactly," Jim agreed. "In our system you can think of the planners as the customers and the employees as the vendors. When the planners see something they want, they communicate it through changes in target scorecards. In a sense, they tell employees what they are willing to pay for it. The employees and their facilitators then figure out how to deliver the specified result."

Edward chimed in. "We planners are the bank's eyes and ears to the outside world," he said. "We determine what new products, territories, technology, or behavior changes the bank needs to stay competitive. We then purchase these from the employees through the performance scorecard system.

"In the old wage-and-hour system, change was extremely difficult. Employee pay was not tied to implementing changes. The employee was paid whether she implemented the change or not. Because pay was not related to performance, we had to rely on subtle, and sometimes not-so-subtle, threats to get change to occur. In this climate of fear, change was difficult to bring about. Intimidation severely reduced employee flexibility and innovation. I suppose you have already heard that?"

"Oh, yes," I said. "I have heard a great deal about the advantages of positive reinforcement compared to aversive control."

Edward nodded agreement and said, "It used to take months to get small changes to occur and years for larger ones. The result was the bank was rarely first into a new market or first to capitalize on new technology. We were always a day late and a dollar short, so to speak. Now we are almost always on the leading edge of change. In today's business environment this responsiveness is a critical advantage for us."

I turned to Jim and said, "I've heard a lot about how employees here are much like self-employed people. But self-employed people don't have planners setting their agendas. It seems to me that they are still directed by the planners, even though it's through the scorecards."

"You make a good point," Jim said. "We tried what's been called 'self-directed workers' early in our performance system conversion. To be successful you need good objectives and good execution. We found out quickly that our employees did not have the knowledge, resources, interest, or time to effectively analyze the marketplace and set objectives. They already had a job. What they were expert at was execution of the plan. We therefore shifted our thinking from self-directed to self-managed workers."

"Further, some of the changes we planners need cross over department lines," Edward explained. "In these cases, our facilitators are an invaluable resource since they work across departments and can see the big picture. After we work with Jim to update the scorecards to match our new objectives, we then work with the facilitators to develop processes that will ensure effective workflow and cooperation across areas."

Edward got out of his chair and moved to a large map of the United States that was hanging on the wall. He pointed to the map and said, "Our long-range plan is to expand our bank to key markets across the country. I'm sure you have heard stories about expansions and acquisitions that were very difficult or even failed."

"Sure," I said.

Edward continued, "Our performance system gives us a unique advantage in this arena. We can communicate our objectives through e-mail and web site scorecards to employees at other locations. Because we don't use managers to communicate, there is substantially less travel and relocation effort and expense than with the old hierarchical management system. When we update the scorecards here, they are automatically and immediately updated everywhere across the country. Of course, in some cases there are unique regional differences that must be considered."

I had not considered the full implications of their management system. Listening to Edward I suddenly became aware of the system's awesome potential. I said, "Managing via scorecards and performance pay really gives you unlimited growth potential. You could locate anywhere in the world through the Internet. It also means that some employees could work at home or anywhere else since you no longer need direct supervisors!"

Edward said, "The flexibility of our new system is simply incredible. It enables us to eliminate the old nine-to-five mentality. People can often set their own hours and in many cases choose the location at which they work. Good ideas like flex-time, job sharing, and working at home never lived up to their potential because they were implemented in organizations with conventional management and compensation."

"I see what you mean," I said. "A company that pays for time can never really have job flexibility. Without measured results to manage by, you can't really let people work at home. For all you know they would spend the day watching television. Linking pay directly to scorecard performance frees the worker and the organization from the restrictions imposed by direct supervision."

"You really get it, I see," Edward said.

"We have a couple of other meetings for Sid," Jim announced. "I really appreciate your spending time with us, Edward."

"You're welcome," he said. "I enjoyed it. Good luck Sid."

"Thanks for everything," I said as we walked toward the door.

Chapter 12

Sid Learns about
The Bank's Transition Experience

"When our owner decided to reengineer the bank's performance system from traditional management and compensation to positive reinforcement, there was a lot of resistance and the change proved difficult. It took several years and a lot of hard work to move away from the old system," Jim explained.

"What kinds of problems?" I asked.

Jim said, "In order of magnitude I would say management resistance, performance constraints, and finally employee resistance."

"What kind of management resistance did you get?" I asked.

Jim explained, "Most people assume that any kind of pay-for-performance scheme will be well accepted by managers and that the buy-in problem will be with staff and production people. To our surprise, this isn't what we found. The managers were the biggest obstacles to the transition. In retrospect, I see why that was so now, but at the time it caught the owner and me by surprise."

"Why were the managers resistant and what did they do to resist?" I asked.

Jim replied, "Well first, let me ask you, who loses the most prestige and financial security if the traditional performance system is replaced?"

I thought a minute. Then it came to me. The manager usually has a much greater investment in the traditional system. She may have gone to business school to prepare for management. Managers have played the game to get where they are in the organization. Managers generally receive higher salaries than workers and often other perks. Why would any manager initially accept a change in the game that she has been so successful at playing?

"Yeah," I said, "I guess the guy making minimum wage has much less to lose than the manager."

"The difference is even greater when you consider that the only immediate way a minimum wage worker can get substantially higher pay is through pay-for-performance," Jim pointed out.

"Okay, I understand the managers have more to risk—what other issues are there?"

Jim replied, "To move away from hierarchical management, subjective performance evaluations, and management by exception requires much more of a change in manager behavior than worker behavior. Managers usually like the traditional system of management better than our system—at least initially."

"They like it better!" I exclaimed.

"Yes, managers are used to traditional management. It's familiar, easy, and it feels good," Jim said with regret in his voice. "They are used to managing this way and are used to being managed this way. It's easier than continually measuring employee performance, providing feedback, and working with employees to improve performance. In the conventional system, all the manager has to do is sit in his office, make sure people show up on time, and apply corrective actions when errors occur. It's the old adage, 'Show up, and don't screw up!' Actually, with respect to employees, there is little real management going on in businesses."

"I generally buy all that," I said. "But what do you mean that management by exception *feels good*?"

Jim answered, "When an employee fails to come to work or makes a significant mistake, the manager begins to manage by criticizing or threatening the employee. Since an unscheduled absence or an error make the manager angry, venting criticism actually feels good to the manager."

I asked, "So that's what you mean by feels good—sort of like kicking a table we bump into?"

"Exactly," Jim agreed, "but there is still more. The conventional annual review is based mostly on the manager's subjective opinions of an employee's performance. The review therefore gives the manager a lot of discretionary power over subordinates. Subordinates pay attention to the manager and try to meet his demands to ensure they get a good performance review. When you transition to direct, objective measurement of employee results, you reduce or even eliminate this type of manager power."

I continued expressing my thought, "The manager can no longer reward those he likes and ignore or punish those he doesn't?"

"You said that; I didn't," Jim said and smiled.

"So the manager loses personal power over employees," I said. "I guess if you've been managing a while this would be a frightening prospect."

"Without a doubt," Jim said. "The *or else* implied in every supervisor and manager request or assignment is removed. The managers may feel they can no longer command and control effectively."

"Well, that's true isn't it?" I asked.

"Yes, there are fewer ways to scare employees into working. But, by indexing employee pay directly to employee performance, we have replaced fear of the manager with an upside opportunity to earn much higher pay. Direct motivation becomes less of a responsibility for managers. We've been looking for motivation in all the wrong places!"

"Cute," I said. I was getting more comfortable with Jim. "So if the manager isn't commanding and controlling, what is he doing?"

Jim responded, "Providing frequent performance feedback, assisting employees in pinpointing constraints to their performances, and then developing strategies for removing these constraints. In our system, the best manager is the one whose employees earn the most money!" Jim exclaimed. "What he isn't doing is serving as a hall monitor or straw boss for his subordinates."

"Is this why you call your managers facilitators rather than managers?" I asked.

"Yes; it's not simply a title change but a true, functional change in the manager's role," Jim replied.

I continued, "And I suppose that since the manager is no longer involved in direct supervision, you don't need as many managers—excuse me, facilitators?"

"Right!" Jim agreed. "In fact the number of employees that reported to a manager used to average around seven to ten. A facilitator can assist as many as one hundred workers."

"Wow!" I exclaimed.

Jim continued, "We once had 70 managers and supervisors for our 600 employees. The manager payroll was around $2.7 million a year. We now have 10 facilitators with a total payroll of $700,000 for a savings of $2 million a year!"

"So your career track is simple, worker to facilitator to planner," I supposed.

Jim frowned, "Not really. There is no vertical career track here. Each person has a job and is paid based on his or her performance and the overall success of the bank. When an employee retires or leaves, we look for an individual who is best qualified for the role—whether they are in or out of the company. There is no special status to planner or facilitator, only special skills."

"Are you saying that everyone at the bank gets the same pay if they perform well?" I asked.

"No," Jim said quickly. "We still have to consider the job market in determining each job's pay opportunity. Jobs that require special training or skills, or for which there are a shortage of employees in the job pool, are paid more for the same level of performance than jobs that are easy to learn or easy to fill."

He continued, "We also have developed lateral career paths. The more skills an employee becomes proficient in, the higher their performance pay opportunity. Finally, we uncapped the profit sharing so that employee pay increases with profitability without limit."

"What did you do to get the managers to change their ways," I asked.

"Well, first we eliminated the traditional annual performance review, merit pay increase, and the practice of rewarding good performance through promotions," Jim explained. "We took these control tools out of the manager's toolbox. Second, just as with employee pay, we eliminated the manager's base salary and replaced it with performance pay. One of the key performance pay measures for our new facilitators is the success of the employees they assist. Third, all new facilitators attended a workshop on positive leadership and performance analysis and improvement. Finally, when we converted senior managers to planners, the facilitators no longer reported directly to the planners."

"I can see that would all be quite an undertaking," I said.

Jim replied, "It was, but even though the transition started out slowly, the acceptance of the managers accelerated quickly once they were used to their new roles. Today, none of them want to return to the old style of management where they and their subordinates were always adversaries."

"You said there were two other obstacles to the transition?" I asked.

Jim responded, "The second big issue, though more process related than behavioral, was to make sure each employee consistently had the potential to perform well. Ensuring this potential is a key role of the facilitators."

"How do you ensure this potential?" I asked.

Jim began, "There are three primary obstacles to optimal employee performance: the opportunity to perform, the capability to perform, and a good job context within which to perform."

"Yes. I discussed these with Ellen," I said.

"Then I'll move on to the last transition issue we faced," Jim continued. "We did encounter some employee resistance to the change, but not near what we had with the managers. We were in for some surprises here too. For example, which employees do you think were the most receptive to the change—the high performers or the poor performers?"

"That's easy, the high performers would have been the most receptive to pay for performance," I replied.

"That's what I expected too," Jim agreed. "But, in fact, many times the high performer in a job position was the most vocal critic."

"What? Did you figure out why?" I asked.

"Who has the most to lose when you eliminate the conventional subjective review, merit increase, and promotion track—the high performer or the poor performer?" Jim asked.

I immediately saw where he was going. "The high performer would have the most to lose. The poor performer is already losing," I said.

"Exactly!" Jim looked at me approvingly. "The high performer is already judged as best. A new way of measuring performance only has a downside. As we talked about earlier this morning, most high performers in a subjective evaluation system are very skilled at pleasing supervisors and playing the game. Poor performers may be poor performers, or it may be that they appear to be poor performers to the manager. They are not socially attractive to him. The only way out for these *poor* performers may be objective measurement."

"How did you get around the concerns of the high performers?" I asked.

Jim continued, "Throughout our employee orientations we stressed that the performance scores were simply a way to calculate performance payments—not grades or judgments about the employee. On a hundred-point scale if your score was 10 that meant that you earned 10 percent of your performance pay opportunity, not that you failed.

We also stressed that our new management philosophy was continuous improvement. The absolute score was much less important than the performance trend."

"What if an employee continued to get poor scores? Wouldn't you have to fire him?" I asked pointedly.

"He would really fire himself because his pay would be too low to continue working in that job," Jim responded.

"That seems rather heartless," I commented.

"Is it better to reduce the earnings of everyone to ensure a poor performer is paid?" Jim responded. "In some cases, we are able to provide training or coaching for poor performers. In other cases, we may be able to transfer them to work at which they perform better."

Section III:

Superior Button's Transition to a Liberated Workplace

Chapter 13

Level I:
Strategic Performance
Scorecard Design Sessions

I called the first design team session for 9:00 a.m. Monday morning. The meeting would be held in the conference room. The design team would consist of me (the CEO and new planner); Julie (the HR director and new performance system manager); Juanita (the QC manager and new facilitator); Larry (the plant manager); Margaret (the CFO); Elaine (the sales manager); and Jim (the consultant).

I opened the meeting by saying, "As you know, Superior Button has fallen on hard times. I have talked to almost everyone about this, so it's now common knowledge. Several weeks ago, a friend of mine told me about a radically different approach to managing an organization. He suggested I visit First National Bank to get a better understanding of it. I did so, and the people there were very open and helpful about what they call their performance system. By the end of my visit, I came to believe the system would work here and put us back on track. Jim is from First National Bank and has agreed to help us get started."

Jim got up and shook hands with each team member. He said, "I want you to know, I really appreciate the chance to work with you. I learned a lot when we implemented our performance system at the bank, and I look forward to learning even more while working with you."

I continued, "Of course everyone knows each other, but I'd like to talk a few minutes about my new role in our performance system and then have Julie and Juanita talk a few minutes about their new roles. Jim has explained that our new performance system will eventually no longer require a management hierarchy in which managers are responsible for traditional command-and-control functions. This would mean that I would no longer serve in the conventional president or CEO role. Instead, my full-time job will be to research the external business environment to determine our strategic course of action.

"I know I've always had a big role in the strategy, but in the past I haven't had the time to gather much factual information. A second major difference in the new approach is the process by which the strategy is implemented. In the past I assigned each of you objectives and budgets that I thought would achieve our strategy. If you felt my objectives or budgets were unrealistic we would discuss revisions until we finally arrived at our plan for the coming year.

"In the new system, I will pass my strategy to Julie, our new performance system manager or PSM. She will then revise our performance system measures, priority weights, and goals to achieve the strategy. She will do this in consultation with you and others. The team coordinators, who are elected by the teams, will explain the revisions to the system when they occur. The facilitator, Juanita, will work with the teams to identify obstacles to meeting the objectives and help remove them."

"I have a question," Julie interjected. "What if an employee requires discipline? Who will determine if he is put on probation, docked some pay, or fired?"

"Excellent question," I responded. "If an employee is suspected of theft, harassment, or is uncooperative, a charge is sent to our new review committee. The committee listens to the evidence and makes a decision. The committee consists of team leaders and some of us, and rotates every two years. If the issue is poor performance, the new pay system will manage that. Would you go ahead and summarize your new role as PSM for the group?"

Julie began, "As PSM, I will be responsible for the design, implementation, and ongoing maintenance of our performance measurement system. The components of the system I will manage are the performance scorecards, monthly performance feedback, and the distribution of performance pay. I'll receive strategy changes from Sid and recommendations from our new facilitator, Juanita, and the CFO."

Larry, the plant manager, asked, "Will a team leader or other employees be allowed to make suggestions to you regarding measures or pay?"

Julie replied, "As I understand it, only the three people I mentioned can make recommendations regarding system changes."

"Why's that?" Larry asked.

Julie continued. "What we are trying to achieve is up to Sid, our planner," she said. "*How* we achieve it is up to the rest of us. An historical problem with performance measurement and performance pay has been that negotiation has become the focus rather that performance improvement.

"Of course, there are a lot of other negotiations in conventional organizations as well. Employees negotiate their job assignments, salaries, performance reviews, and promotions. Similar negotiations, with respect to performance measures and goals, will undermine the system's integrity and ability to achieve the organization's strategic goals. Further, allowing such negotiations creates inequities across jobs and departments. All performance system changes will be guided by the impact on the strategy, the impact on other employees or departments, and the performance improvement potential."

I spoke up, "Thanks, Julie. Juanita, would you summarize your new facilitator role for us?"

Juanita got up from her seat and went to the white board. She wrote the following formula.

$$Performance = Opportunity + Capability + Context$$

Juanita began, "My job is to increase organizational success through assisting the teams in maximizing their performances and their performance pay. I will review performance trends each month to pinpoint performances that are consistently below goal or trending in the wrong direction. I will then meet with the relevant team or teams to pinpoint possible obstacles to performance improvement. In some cases, the problem may be the performance measure itself or an invalid goal. In these cases I will consult with Julie and Sid to determine the systemic impact of a revision.

"However, in most cases, the obstacle will likely be either lack of opportunity, lack of capability, or an unsupportive job context. Examples of a lack of opportunity are delayed or poor quality work input, excess staffing, or a lack of cross-training. Examples of a lack of capability are ineffective employee selection, inadequate training, insufficient staffing, and inefficient work processes or workflow. Finally, the day-to-day job context may not support performance improvement. This is typically due to poor coordination and performance management. In this case I will initially work with the current managers and supervisors to improve their performance management skills. Some obstacles may require initiatives that include several areas. I will then be working with a group of team coordinators to overcome these obstacles."

Margaret, the CFO, spoke up for the first time. "Wow, you're going to be really busy!"

"Looks like it," Juanita agreed. "But it's really what I'm interested in and good at."

I then said, "Margaret, why don't you tell us about your role as CFO in our new performance system."

Margaret nodded yes and said, "Well, I still will have my current financial reporting duties. However, I'll be working closely with Sid in defining strategic changes, with Julie regarding measure data availability and goal setting, and with Juanita when she is developing improvement plans that involve financial data. I guess I'd say, I will have the same functions but will be able to carry them out in a different manner."

"Elaine, tell us about your role in the new system," I requested.

"Well, I think it will be about the same except I'll be working with you to determine what to sell, and when, and with Juanita if I have salespeople who are not meeting their quotas. I have a question though, what's going to happen to my peoples' sales commissions?"

I replied, "I don't really know. Do you have any ideas, Jim?"

Jim nodded and said, "Elaine, would you describe the sales commission plan for me?"

Elaine explained, "They get five percent of each month's gross sales once they pass their thresholds. It's a simple plan and we've had it for almost five years."

Jim asked, "How is each salesperson's threshold decided on?"

Elaine responded, "They are based on the salesperson's experience. The more experienced salesperson is given a higher threshold."

Jim tried not to show his concern, but it was obvious he had problems with the sales commission plan. "Are you on commission also?"

"Yes, and I have the highest threshold," Elaine said proudly.

Jim replied, "I think we can make some adjustments to the commission plan that will improve it. Margaret, do your different product lines yield different margins?"

"Yes, the gross margins vary with the type of material and the amount of material purchased at discount. These margins run from 6 percent all the way to 22 percent."

Jim continued, "Gross sales as a commission measure doesn't consider each product's margin. It would be better to pay commissions on gross profit rather than gross sales so salespeople would focus on products with high margins. Would you agree, Elaine?"

Elaine responded, "Makes sense to me. I didn't realize how widely the margins vary among product lines. We'll make the adjustment right away!"

"Hold on!" Jim exclaimed. "There may be other things to consider before we implement a new plan. Salespeople often have a big impact on other aspects of the company. For example, what happens to a sales commission if the customer doesn't make the payments or pays late?"

Embarrassed, Elaine replied, "Nothing."

Jim responded, "Don't you want your salespeople to make sure they sell to people who can and will pay you, and don't you want them to continue to be interested in how quickly they pay after the sale?"

"Of course," Elaine said defensively.

"Okay, one solution would be to pay them only on collected revenue. Another would be to develop a multiple-measure sales scorecard," Jim explained. We can decide the better approach after we talk more."

Jim continued, "Three other possible issues in sales, besides gross margin and collections, are customer service, order accuracy and timeliness, and inventory. Is it important that your salespeople not only sell to customers but also visit customers and help identify and solve their problems?"

I interrupted, "You bet! We have a limited number of customers who order from us on a fairly regular basis. If we lose one of them, the revenue and replacement costs are substantial."

Jim responded, "So, some way of assessing customer satisfaction would be an important salesperson measure?"

Elaine and I responded simultaneously, "Yes!"

Jim continued, "Order accuracy and timeliness refer to a group of sales behaviors. These include writing up the order accurately, submitting it quickly, and ensuring promises made to customers can be delivered completely and on time. Are any of these issues for your sales group?"

Elaine said, "The orders have been accurate and the commission ensures they are submitted quickly. However, we do have incidents where a customer receives an incomplete order or the order delivery is late. I know this, because the irate customer calls me rather than the salesperson. Most of the time however, it's late or incomplete because manufacturing doesn't deliver."

Larry, the plant manager, spoke up loudly, "What? We could deliver if your salespeople didn't make impossible promises to customers without checking with us first!"

I interrupted, "Settle down everybody."

Jim said, "A customer order is always a cooperative effort between sales and production. I'm not saying it happens here, but it is common for manufacturing to reduce its workload by providing incomplete shipments or stretching out delivery times. On the other hand, it is also common for salespeople, in the heat of the moment, to make promises that can't be met by production.

"One strategy for rewarding cooperation is to cross-link scorecard measures. For example, salespeople could be measured on production's timeliness and order accuracy measures, while the production scorecard would include sales gross profit and customer satisfaction. It would look like this." Jim went to the board and drew the following:

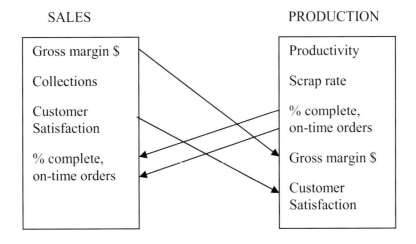

Elaine studied the diagram and said, "Maybe it's worth thinking about developing a scorecard for the salespeople."

I said, "Thanks everybody. It's clear to me that everyone understands their new roles and that the commission plan may need revision. Jim, why don't you take over and explain the design and implementation process you used at the bank."

Jim went to the board and erased Juanita's formula. He then wrote the following list.

Major Tasks
1. Scorecard Design
2. Performance Pay Design
3. Data Management Development
4. Communications
5. Performance Facilitation Training
6. Implementation of Performance Improvement Projects

"This is the general order of design and implementation for the first transition Level I recommend," Jim stated flatly.

Julie asked, "Shouldn't we explain the system to everyone first so they know what is going on?"

Jim responded, "At the bank we found it was a bad idea to present the system as a bunch of concepts. Employees became apprehensive and began guessing as to what we were up to. Better to design the system first and present the actual trial measures and performance pay opportunity. The good news is that the initial design process can be accomplished in a few weeks if everyone does their part. I suggest we begin the scorecard design process next Monday morning,"

"You're kidding!" Julie exclaimed. "We just found out about the system in the last few days. We're not ready!" she said, clearly agitated.

"Will we be any more ready six months from now?" Jim asked.

Julie responded, "Sure, Sid would have time to develop a strategy, I could finish my class, Larry and Margaret could make sure we have the data management system we will need. There are a lot of loose ends here!"

Jim replied, "You've got to get on a bike to learn how to ride it. You will come to understand the system fully only when you start working with the nuts and bolts of the system. We will test and revise the measures during a trial period."

"I agree with Jim's view," I spoke up. "Also, let's not forget what prompted all this. Superior Button is in financial trouble. If we wait too long, there won't be an organization to design a system for!"

The design team met in the conference room on Monday morning. Everyone sat around a modest-sized conference table. There was a whiteboard on the wall and a flipchart in the corner. The aroma of freshly brewed coffee filled the air.

Jim stood and said, "Our first order of business is to develop the company's strategic scorecard. There are seven performance dimensions we should be concerned about. Four of these dimensions drive short-term profitability and three drive long-term profitability." Jim went to the whiteboard and drew the following table. "These seven measurement categories were arrived at statistically by clustering thousands of measures into the smallest number of groupings."

	Short-term Profitability				Long-term Profitability		
Area	Sales	Expense	Productivity	Cash Flow	Regulatory Compliance	Customer Satisfaction	Special Projects
Company							
Finance							
HR							
Sales							
Warehouse							
Cutting							
Finishing							
Packing							
Shipping							
Order Entry							

Jim continued, "Let me explain the performance dimensions to you so we can get started. Sales are typically expressed as total revenue. Four employee behaviors affect sales: prospecting, closing, up-selling, and cross-selling. These measures may apply as we move down through the organization. However the organizational measure will be **total revenue**.

"Expenses divided by revenue is the typical overall expense measure and includes only expenses that are actionable by employees. The numerator of the ratio is the sum of controllable expenses. *Expenses are defined as a ratio since the ones that are controllable typically increase and decrease with revenue or workload.* The typical expenses the employees impact are selling, production, and delivery expenses, although there may be others. The organizational measure will be **controllable expenses / revenue**.

"Labor cost is separated out from other types of expenses as *productivity* because the improvement strategies are different. Labor cost is also compared to revenue since workload affects it. Four sub-categories of productivity are efficiency, utilization, rework, and throughput. These measures will take a more prominent role as we cascade down through the organization. Our organizational productivity measure will be **labor expense / revenue**.

"Cash flow is largely made up of receivables, inventory, and payables. Different businesses' cash flow is driven by one or more of these categories. When a business is impacted by all three, the aggregate measure *working capital efficiency* is useful. What are the employee controllable aspects of cash flow at Superior Button?"

Margaret, the CFO, stated, "We don't have any real problems with receivables since we have only a few customers and they have done business with us for years. We do have a sizeable raw materials inventory, however, and improvements could be made. Our payables are under control—we pay at the last possible date."

Jim concluded, "Sounds like inventory is the organizational cash-flow issue. Two measures are inventory turns and DIO—Days Inventory Outstanding. Which do you prefer?"

Margaret responded, "I prefer DIO."

Jim continued, "Our organizational cash-flow measure will be DIO. Regulatory compliance can be measured a number of ways. Compliance relates to federal and state agencies as well as trade and internal compliance issues. Which of these are important to Superior Button?"

Larry replied, "We are most concerned with OSHA and safety issues. There are a lot of ways to get hurt in the plant. We are also interested in ISO 9000 certification."

Jim thought a minute and said, "At the organizational level, I prefer to measure recordable incidents for OSHA. Since ISO 9000 is a project, it would make sense to measure it as a special project."

I piped up, "I've heard that if you pay incentives for a reduction in accidents, employees may simply not report them. If this happened, it would put them and us at risk!"

Jim replied, "I agree that we don't want to measure accidents on the employee scorecards," Jim nodded. "We will most likely score employees through an internal safety audit in which safe practices are observed each month. No one's performance pay is affected by the organizational scorecard. Its purposes are to serve as a blueprint for all scorecard design throughout the organization. It then becomes a means for evaluating and revising the program once the system is in place."

Jim continued, "It's settled, then. We'll measure regulatory compliance as *number of recordable safety incidents per 10,000 labor hours* and progress on ISO 9000 as a *special project*. Is that okay?"

"Yes," everyone said in unison.

"I think we should measure customer satisfaction as account attrition on the organizational scorecard," Jim suggested. "After all, that is the bottom line. Do you currently measure account attrition?"

Larry and Margaret spoke at the same time. "No, we don't. How would you measure it?"

Jim said, "One fairly simple way is to look at the percentage of accounts that have made no purchases in the past so many days. You can look at the typical purchasing activity of your current accounts to decide on how many days. A more sophisticated way would be to compute the average purchase cycle for each client and compare current purchasing to this standard."

Jim continued, "One drawback to these measures is that they are lagging rather than leading indicators. This problem, however, can be handled in the design of the lower-level scorecard measures."

Margaret spoke, "Let's use the more sophisticated one. We don't have that many customers to track and it would give us an early warning system if something was wrong!"

"Great!" Jim agreed. "Our customer service measure will be *percent accounts not purchasing on time.*

"Our last dimension is special projects," he said, obviously pleased with the progress we were making. "The criteria for these projects are that they are of fairly long duration, not a part of a person's typical job responsibilities, and they are developmental for the organization so their impact is in the future. Do you have any such projects other than ISO 9000?"

"Not really," I said worried. "Given what you've said, I guess we probably should have such projects."

"We're too busy as it is!" Julie exclaimed.

Jim replied, "Perhaps such projects will develop given your new roles. This would be true especially in the planning and facilitation roles. But for now, I suggest we only include ISO 9000 on your organizational scorecard. We'll track project-milestone accuracy and timeliness.

"Our goal today was to complete the company row of this table by defining performance measures and priority weights for each cell in the company row," Jim explained. "Each measure below the company level will be selected based on its impact on its related company measure."

I said, "What if we have other issues than these? For example, I am interested in my return on equity which isn't on the list."

Jim replied, "These measurement dimensions were selected based upon the ability of employees to affect them. There are of course dozens of financial indicators that are valuable in determining the success or value of a company. However, these indicators are not necessarily related to employee performance. For example, how much direct control do employees have over your equity?"

"None," I said reluctantly. "But surely net income should be on the list."

Jim said, "First, net income includes a lot of factors that employees don't directly control. For example, the cost of raw materials, rent, taxes, and loan interest aren't really controlled by employee performance. Second, net income is an aggregate measure that really doesn't direct specific performances or pinpoint improvement opportunities. Third, when we design the performance pay system we will index all payouts to net income to ensure the pay is affordable and that the performance measures and payouts are self-regulating."

"What do you mean by self-regulating?" I asked.

Jim replied, "Indexing all performance pay, and eventually all pay, to profit or net income ensures that payments will only be made when profit actually improves. As a result, if we measure the wrong things, or set the wrong goals, employees may score well on their scorecards but there will be no profit improvement to share. Put simply, 100 percent of nothing is still nothing!"

I continued, "So, if I set the wrong strategy, or Julie measures the wrong things, the measurements won't have any effect on profits and no one will get any money?"

"Pretty much," Jim said. "But the factors they can't control will also affect their payouts."

You mean like the rent, cost of raw materials, and so on?" I asked.

"Yes," said Jim.

"That doesn't seem fair to me," I said, concerned. "The employees don't make those decisions, so why should they be penalized or rewarded for them?"

Jim responded, "The alternative is that you would have to pay them when there is insufficient profit to make the payments.

"I see," I agreed. "We can't share what we don't have is what you are saying."

"Right," Jim said. "Besides ensuring a sustainable system, indexing pay to the company profit may, in some cases, encourage employees to come up with ideas that might improve uncontrollable expenses."

Jim went to the board and drew a new table with the organizational measures.

Area	Sales	Expense	Productivity	Cash Flow	Regulatory Compliance	Customer Satisfaction	Special Projects
Company	Revenue	Expenses / Revenue	Labor Cost / Revenue	DIO	Recordables/ 10,000 hours	Account Attrition percent	ISO 9000 Milestones
Priority Weight							

He then drew the following table below it.

Measure	Economic Impact	Improvement Opportunity	Ease of Improvement	Total
Revenue				
Expenses/Revenue				
Labor Cost/Revenue				
DIO				
Total Recordables				
Account Attrition				
ISO 9000 Milestones				

Rating Scale

4 = High   2 = Moderately Low

3 = Moderately High   1 = Low

Jim turned around and said, "I want each of you to rate each measure in terms of the economic impact of an improvement, how much opportunity to improve you believe there is, and how much effort and cost would be involved in generating an improvement. I'd like you to rate independently and write your ratings on a scrap of paper. I'll ask you for them in a few minutes."

"What if we're not sure about some of the dimensions?" Julie asked.

Jim responded, "All of you have worked here for some time and have general impressions. That is all I am asking for at this point— your impressions."

Jim left the room to call his bank while everyone else begin to rate the company performance measures. When he returned, everyone was finished.

"Good work," Jim announced. "Now I'm going to ask each of you to give me your ratings which I'll put on the board."

Jim asked each person for their ratings and filled in the table.

Measure	Economic Impact	Improvement Opportunity	Ease of Improvement	% of Total
Revenue	4,4,3,4,3,4 = 22	4,3,4,4,4,3 = 22	2,3,2,1,1,2 = 11	55 15.9%
Expenses / Revenue	2,2,1,3,4,2 = 14	3,3,3,3,3,3 = 18	4,3,4,4,3,2 = 20	52 15.0%
Labor Cost / Revenue	4,2,4,4,4,2 = 20	4,4,4,3,4 3 = 22	1,4,3,4,3,4 = 19	61 17.6%
DIO	2,2,1,1,1,1 = 8	2,3,3,1,2,2 = 13	3,3,4,4,3,3 = 20	41 11.8%
Total Incidents	2,2,2,2,1,1 = 10	4,4,4,3,4,2 = 21	3,2,4,2,3,2 = 16	47 13.5%
Account Attrition	4,4,4,4,4,4 = 24	3,2,4,3,4,2 = 18	4,4,2,4,2,2 = 18	60 17. 3%
ISO 9000 Milestones	2,1,1,2,2,4 = 12	2,3,2,1,1,1 = 10	1,1,2,1,2,2 =9	31 8.9%
				347 100. 0%

Jim said, "Let me round these to simplify the weightings." The table then became

Measure	Percent
Revenue	15%
Expenses/Revenue	15%
Labor Cost/Revenue	20%
DIO	10%
Total Recordables	15%
Account Attrition	15%
ISO 9000 Milestones	10%
TOTAL	**100%**

"Do these priority weightings look about right?" Jim asked.

I responded, "I don't think these weightings adequately reflect our major problem—margin."

"An interesting result of this exercise is that it reflects the perceptions of the management group—not always the reality," Jim pointed out. "Sid, how would you reweight the list given your new planner role?"

I said, "I'd take five from customer satisfaction—we don't have a serious problem with that now. I'd move it to expenses. Then I'd take five from compliance and move it to productivity for the same reason. Finally, I would take five from cash flow and move it to revenue.

"Okay. Our list looks like this," Jim revised the list again.

Measure	Percent
Revenue	15% + 5% = 20%
Expenses/Revenue	15% + 5% = 20%
Labor Cost/Revenue	20% + 5% = 25%
DIO	10% - 5% = 5%
Total Incidents	15% - 5% = 10%
Account Attrition	15% - 5% = 10%
ISO 9000 Milestones	10% = 10%
	TOTAL 100%

"What does everybody think?" Jim asked.

Larry said, "Well, the emphasis is more on short-term profitability, as it should be. Now 70 percent of the total weighting is on short-term profits."

Jim explained, "When your situation changes, you may want to change the weights to have a more balanced set of priorities with respect to long- and short-term profitability. But given your present situation, I believe these priorities are valid."

I was silently pleased with the results of the session. Our executive team was now properly focused on the short-term margin issue. I was concerned about the low weights for compliance and customer satisfaction he had assigned, but realized they would need to take a back seat to revenue, expenses, and productivity for the remainder of this year at any rate.

Chapter 14

Level I: Executive Performance Scorecard Design Session

The design team met the following day in the same room. Yesterday's session had taken about three hours. Everyone seemed interested and ready to continue.

Jim began, "Today, we begin the process of cascading the scorecards down through the organization. First, we will design your scorecards in this meeting. Then, I'll work with each of you to continue drilling down the scorecards to your direct reports and finally their direct reports. We'll cascade the measures using the current organizational reporting structure. This structure will change as we transition to higher levels which will likely change some of the scorecards."

"At the executive level, it is important that we design each person's scorecard as a group. In this way, we can ensure the measures complement each other across areas and that they truly reflect the company strategic scorecard measures and priorities. After this meeting, however, all the remaining scorecards will only involve the division head, the subordinate manager, Julie, and Sid."

Larry spoke up. "I don't see how we can duplicate the company scorecard at every level. Some employees have no impact on some of the measures. This becomes even more the case as we begin moving down through the organization."

"Good point," Jim replied. "For each job position, we will discuss how it might affect each of the performance measures the next level up. In some cases, there will be no connection and that dimension will be skipped. In other cases, a job may affect the next level up, but a more specific and actionable measure for that job level will be substituted." Jim went to the white board and drew the following table.

Manager	Job Position	Revenue	Expenses/ Revenue	Labor Cost/ Revenue	DIO	Total Recordables	Account Attrition	ISO 9000 Mile-stones
	Company	Revenue	Expenses/ Revenue	Labor Cost/ Revenue	DIO	Total Recordables	Account Attrition	Mile-stones
		15%	20%	25%	10%	10%	10%	10%
Sid	CEO							
Julie	HR Director							
Larry	Plant Manager							
Margaret	CFO							
Elaine	Sales Manager							
Juanita	QA Manager							

"Let's begin with Sid," Jim said. As the new planner which company measures do you affect?"

I thought a minute and said, "Well, my market research should affect both revenue and account attrition. I'll also be looking into new technology and processes that could reduce some expenses and improve productivity. I don't think I will have much impact on the other measures, through."

"Does everyone agree or have any comments?" Jim asked the group.

"I don't claim to fully understand Sid's new role yet, but these seem like the right measures," Margaret agreed.

"Sid, how would you priority weight your measures?" Jim asked.

I replied, "I'd put 30 percent on revenue and 30 percent on productivity and then 20 percent on expenses and 20 percent on account attrition."

"Fine," Jim replied. Our new table looks like this."

Manager	Job Position	Revenue	Expenses/ Revenue	Labor Cost / Revenue	DIO	Total Recordables	Account Attrition	ISO 9000 Mile-stones
	Company	Revenue 15%	Expenses / Revenue 20%	Labor Cost / Revenue 25%	DIO 10%	Total Recordables 10%	Account Attrition 10%	Mile-stones 10%
Sid	CEO	30%	20%	30%			20%	
Julie	HR Director							
Larry	Plant Manager							
Margaret	CFO							
Elaine	Sales Manager							
Juanita	QA Manager							

The design team continued down the table designing measures for each member. At 4:00 p.m. all of the executive scorecards were designed.

Manager	Job Position	Revenue	Expenses/ Revenue	Labor Cost/ Revenue	DIO	Total Recordables	Account Attrition	ISO 9000 Milestones
	Company	Monthly Revenue 15%	Expenses /Revenue 20%	Labor Cost/ Revenue 25%	DIO 10%	Total Recordables 10%	Account Attrition 10%	Milestones Met 10%
Sid	CEO	Monthly Revenue 30%	Expense/ Revenue 20%	Labor/ Revenue 30%			Account Attrition 20%	
Julie	HR Director		Hiring Expense /Hire 20%	Days to Fill a Hire 20% Hires completing Probation 20% Unforced Employee Attrition 30%		6MMA number of grievances 10%		
Juanita	QA Manager		Expense / Revenue 10%	Labor Cost / Revenue 30%	DIO 10%	Total Recordables 20%		ISO 9000 Milestones Met 30%

continued

Larry	Plant Manager	Monthly Revenue 10%	Scrap 15 % Maint. Expense/ lb. 15%	Labor cost / lb. 20%	DIO 10%	6MMA # of Safety Incidents 10%	Orders on time 10% Returns 10%	ISO 9000 Milestones Met 10%
Margaret	CFO	Reports on time 20% Average Budget variance 25%		DIO 15%			Accurate billings 15% Vendor payments on time 15%	ISO 9000 milestones met 10%
Elaine	Sales Manager	Monthly Revenue 50%	Gross Margin 20%	Sales Labor / Revenue 10%	DIO 5%		Account Attrition 15%	

I said, "I'm surprised at how efficiently we developed the table. It's probably flawed in some ways, but it is really a good start."

Julie chimed in, "I was pretty skeptical, as you all know, but I agree with Jim that going through this exercise now clarifies the process for me."

Larry said, "It now seems like all this is really doable!"

Finally, Margaret said, "I like what I see, but where are the goals? What percent of reports should be on time, how close to budget should we be, and so forth?"

Jim said, "Good point, Margaret. The next step in the process is to develop mins and maxes for each of the measures. Before we get into that, however, you need to understand that we will be using the performance matrix format to organize each job position's scorecard measures. The matrix uses percent gain to measure progress rather than percent goal. Percent gain is the percentage a measure's performance has moved from a min to a max. It's computed like this."

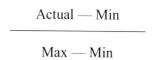

$$\frac{\text{Actual} - \text{Min}}{\text{Max} - \text{Min}}$$

"What's wrong with percent of goal?" asked Margaret. "We've always used it before."

Jim responded, "Percent goal has some inherent math problems since there is no lower limit with which to compare. For example, if Margaret is at 90 percent of goal on reports on time, would that be acceptable?"

Margaret said softly, "Well no, that would mean 10 out of a hundred reports are either inaccurate or late. That would be totally unacceptable."

Jim nodded in agreement and said, "If we set a min of 80 and a max of 100 then the percent gain for 90 would look like this."

$$\frac{90 - 80}{100 - 80} = 50\%$$

"Margaret, would you agree that you should earn 50 percent of your performance pay by achieving 90 percent on time and accurate?" Jim asked.

"Not really," Margaret replied.

"Okay, let's set the min at 90 percent and see what happens," Jim continued.

$$\frac{90 - 90}{100 - 90} = 0\%$$

"With a min of 90 percent, 90 percent on-time would yield a score of zero. You would not receive any incentive pay for this level of performance," Jim explained. He continued, "At 95 percent on time you would earn 50 percent and at 100 percent you would earn 100 percent."

"I see," Margaret said. "Yes, I agree that percent gain is a better way of judging performance than a simple percent of goal."

"Good," Jim said. "Your assignments for our next meeting are to define a min and max for each of your measures. I recommend you work together on measures that are shared.

"Let me give you some tips for setting min and max," Jim went on. *Min* is defined as current or minimally acceptable performance. *Max* is defined as what the company needs to meet its goals with reasonable expectations. Well-designed mins and maxes will yield initial percent gains of 30 percent to 70 percent. It is unwise to set the min or max so high that everyone scores zero. On the other hand, if the min and max are too easy, everyone will get 100 percent and there will be no reinforcement for improvement."

I asked, "So what is an *A* and what is an *F* in this system?"

Jim seemed upset by my question. He asked, "Why would you want to assign a grade? A score of 50 percent simply means you get 50 percent of the performance pay for the measure. The scorecards are not really evaluations. They are a means of sharing profits with those who help earn them. As a self-employed entrepreneur, do you think of yourself in terms of letter grades?"

I said embarrassed, "No, I'm either making money or I'm not. Forget what I asked; it's clearly old-school thinking. No pun intended."

Jim announced, "Let's meet again next Thursday. That will give you over a week to set your mins and maxes. They can be modified during the test period, so don't agonize over perfection. I'd like Sid and Margaret to decide on the company mins and maxes and bring them along with their own."

The following Thursday the group reconvened in the conference room. Everyone had their mins and maxes with them. Jim added them to the measurement table.

Company and Executive Performance Scorecards

Job Position	Revenue	Expenses /Revenue	Labor Cost / Revenue	DIO	Total Incidents	Account Attrition	ISO 9000 Milestones
Company	Monthly Revenue 15% MN=$400,000 MX=$500,000	Target Exps /Rev 20% MN=18% MX=12%	Labor Cost / Revenue 25% MN=57% MX=35%	DIO 10% MN=60 MX=40	Total Recordables 10% MN=1 MX=0	Account Attrition 10% MN=18% MX12%	Milestones Met 10% MN=70% MX=100%
CEO Sid	Monthly Revenue 30% MN=$400,000 MX=$500,000	Target Exp / Rev 20% MN=18% MX=12%	Labor Cost / Revenue 30% MN=57% MX=35%			Account Attrition 20% MN=18% MX=12%	
HR Director Julie		Hiring expense / employee 20% MN=$450 MX=$300	Days to fill a hire 20% MN=40 days MX=20 days New hires completing probation 20% MN= 70% MX=90% Unforced Emp. Attrition. 30% MN=12% MX= 4%		6MMA number of grievances 10% MN= 2.0 MX= .5		
Plant Manager Larry	Monthly Revenue 10% MN=$400,000 MX=$500,000	Scrap 15% MN=17% MX=5% Maint Exp / Pound 15% MN=$8.00 MX=$6.00	Labor cost / Pound 20% MN=$120 MX=$90	DIO 5% MN=60 MX=40	6MMA Average number of safety incidents 10% MN=1.5 MX=.5	Orders on time 10% MN=74% MX=100% Returns 10% MN=7% MX= 3%	ISO 9000 milestones met 10% MN=70% MX= 100%
CFO Margaret		Accurate reports on time 20% MN=95% MX=100% Avg Budget variance 25% MN=12% MX=5%		DIO 15% MN=60 MX=40		Accurate billings 15% MN=97% MX=100% Vendor payments on time 15% MN=87% MX=95%	ISO 9000 milestones met 10% MN=70% MX= 100%
Sales Elaine	Monthly Revenue 50% MN=$400,000 MX=$500,000	Gross Margin 20% MN=18% MX=24%	Sales Labor / Revenue 10% MN=14% MX=12%	DIO 5% MN=60 MX=40		Account Attrition 15% MN=18% MX=12%	
Juanita		Target Expense / Revenue 10% MN= 18% MX= 12%	Labor Cost / Revenue 30% MN= 57% MX= 35%	DIO 10% MN=60 MX=40	Total Recordables 20% MN=1 MX= 0		ISO 9000 Milestones Met 30% MN= 70% MX= 100%

Jim exclaimed, "Great job, everyone. I know you spent some time working together on the measures you had in common. What's your opinion, Sid?"

I answered, "It looks like an ambitious start, which is what we need!"

"Good," Jim said. "Next Tuesday let's meet so that I can explain the rest of the measurement process and we can set up a design session schedule with the other managers."

Chapter 15

Level I: Cascading Scorecards Down Through the Organization

A few weeks passed and Jim was ready to meet with the middle managers and supervisors to complete the remaining scorecard design process. Jim had been given an organizational chart to help him understand what scorecards remained to be developed.

Superior Button Organizational Chart

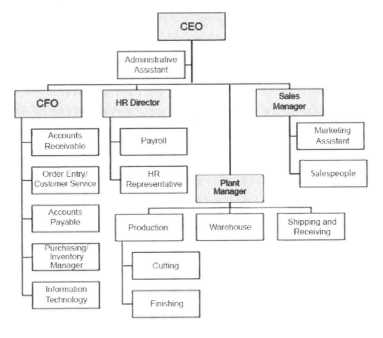

The first lower-level scorecard design meeting included all of the managers. Jim began, "In defining the measures, we will apply the following criteria." Jim went to the board and wrote the following list.

Performance Measure Criteria
Objective
Result
Individual or small team
Actionable
Aligned
Balanced
Timely
One element
Third party

Jim continued. "By objective, I mean a tangible, quantifiable result—not an opinion. "A result means that the measures always refer to some outcome that is of value to the organization, not the process by which the result is obtained. Though everything begins with employee behavior, scorecard measures will almost always be results. For example, *number of sales calls completed* is a behavior. The result is *number of sales or sales revenue.*

"At your level in the organization, you are responsible for large outcomes. However, as we move down toward workers, another criterion will be that all measures refer to small teams of no more than 10 employees or individual performances. Research finds that measures that relate to the collective performances of a large group are ineffective at improving or sustaining performance. Put simply, too many cooks spoil the broth!

"A key criterion for selecting a measure is whether it is actionable by the employee or employees to which it is assigned. There is simply no reason to measure someone on something they can't do anything to improve.

"All scorecard measures, at every level, should reflect the strategy described by the company scorecard. We want alignment in our measurement system—everyone rowing their oars in the same direction.

"Because the strategy is multidimensional, it is also critical that each scorecard's measures are balanced. We don't want improvements in one performance dimension to reduce performance in other equally important dimensions. For example, we don't want to increase sales revenue at the expense of margin or customer satisfaction. We don't want production to increase at the expense of safety, expense, or quality. Each time we select a performance measure we will ask the question, 'What adverse impact could occur if the employee focused only on this measure?' If there could be a significant problem, we will add a measure that addresses the issue.

"We also want measures for which the data can be collected in a timely fashion. The data for any measure we select should be available at least monthly, if not more often."

Jim continued, "Aggregated measures such as profit, total expenses, and so on do not direct or guide specific employee behaviors. These measures make some sense at the management level, but at the worker level it is better to target specific components of the aggregation. Similarly, complex ratios and percentages can sometimes be poor measures. It is best to try to focus each measure on one element and a specific set of employee behaviors.

"Third-party measures are measures for which the data are collected by someone other than the performer. In general, self-reported data, that cannot be audited should not be used to determine performance pay. Self-reported data provides excellent feedback. Probably the best answer is to weight self-reported data zero so that it does not affect the employee's performance pay, but does provide feedback that relates to a payout measure. For example, salespeople could self-report number of sales calls made, but would be paid on actual sales."

Jim asked, "Which area would like to be the first area to develop their scorecards?"

Larry, the plant manager, responded, "I'd like my area to start first today."

Jim said, "Okay. We'll continue the meeting with Larry and his managers and supervisors. Julie will set up meetings with the other areas for later this week."

Jim went to the board and put up Larry's scorecard which was designed in the executive session.

Job Position	Measure	Min	Max	Priority Weight
Plant Manager	Monthly Revenue	$400,000	$500,000	10%
	Scrap Expense / Revenue	17%	5%	10%
	Maintenance Expense / Pound	$8.00	$6.00	15%
	Labor Cost / Pound	$12.00	$9.00	20%
	DIO	60 days	40 days	5%
	6MMA # of Safety Incidents	1.5	.5	10%
	% Orders On Time	74%	100%	10%
	% Returns	7%	3%	10%
	% ISO 9000 Milestones Met	70%	100%	10%

"Which job will we start with, Larry?" Jim asked.

"I think I'd like to work backwards and start with shipping. Is that good for you, Susan?"

Designing the Shipping Manager's Performance Scorecard

Susan, the shipping manager, nodded her head yes.

Jim explained, "The design process will be to decide which measures on Larry's scorecard a specific job impacts. The measures may not be the same, but will always drive Larry's scorecard results which, in turn, drive the company scorecard. This way, all the measures will be aligned and will drive the company strategy.

"Who do you manage, Susan?" As Susan described each job, Jim wrote them below Larry's scorecard.

Susan–Shipping Manager

Tom–Loading Supervisor

Ed–Transportation Supervisor

Alice–Production Manager

Ahmed–Warehouse Manager

Jim continued, "Susan, let's design your scorecard first. Look at each of Larry's measures and tell me if there are any that don't relate to your area or are defined too broadly."

Job Position	Measure	Min	Max	Priority Weight
Plant Manager	**Monthly Revenue**	**$400,000**	**$500,000**	**10%**
	Scrap Expense / Revenue	17%	5%	10%
	Maintenance Expense / Pound	$8.00	$6 00	15%
	Labor Cost / Pound	$12.00	$9.00	20%
	DIO	60 days	40 days	5%
	6MMA # of Safety Incidents	1.5	.5	10%
	% Orders On Time	74%	100%	10%
	% Returns	7%	3%	10%
	% ISO 9000 Milestones Met	70%	100%	10%

Susan quickly said, "We don't really affect sales or revenue in any direct way."

Jim replied, "Any time an employee has contact with customers there is a potential sales opportunity. Do any of your employees come in contact with customers?"

"Well, our drivers come in contact with them, but I don't see how they can sell anything," Susan said with skepticism.

"When the driver unloads his delivery, does he talk to a customer's manager or other employees?" Jim asked

"Yes," Susan replied.

Jim continued, "Does he go into the customer's warehouse when he's unloading?"

"Sometimes," Susan said.

Jim asked, "When he's talking with the customer could he ask them if any of their inventories are low? Or, when he's in the warehouse, could he take a look and see if the inventories we provide are low?"

Ed, the driver supervisor spoke up. "What you're asking is possible, but my drivers are too busy unloading to do any selling. Also, they would have to be trained in what to ask or how to spot low inventories."

Jim said, "I don't believe asking the customer whether he needs anything, or looking at your inventories in the customer's warehouse, would take much time. As to the training, that might be needed—it's hard to say right now."

Larry spoke, "The company has a revenue problem. I think we should pursue this."

Susan said, "You're going to measure me, Ed, and our drivers on selling! This is not what drivers are responsible for. Their job is to make sure deliveries are on time!"

Jim replied, "Remember, the logic of the system is to identify key results that drive the company's success. The measures are not so much what we are doing as they are what we should be doing. If we keep doing exactly the same things, how much profit improvement would you expect?"

Susan said, heatedly, "It's just not fair to reduce a driver's performance pay because they don't sell anything!"

"Susan," Jim replied, "Remember that the company can only afford additional pay if profits improve. If we don't measure things that actually improve profit, then everyone will simply get 100 percent of nothing!"

Susan dejectedly said, "Okay, add revenue to my scorecard."

Shipping Mgr.	Monthly Revenue	$400,000	$500,000	10%

Jim pointed out, "The next category on Larry's scorecard is scrap. Is this measure relevant to your area, Susan?"

Job Position	Measure	Min	Max	Priority Weight
Plant Manager	Monthly Revenue	$400,000	$500,000	10%
	Scrap Expense / Revenue	**17%**	**5%**	**10%**
	Maintenance Expense / Pound	$8. 00	$6.00	15%
	Labor Cost / Pound	$12.00	$9.00	20%
	DIO	60 days	40 days	5%
	6MMA # of Safety Incidents	1.5	.5	10%
	% Orders On Time	74%	100%	10%
	% Returns	7%	3%	10%
	% ISO 9000 Milestones Met	70%	100%	10%

Susan answered, "Well, not the total scrap, only some aspects of it. They can waste materials or package items in boxes that are too big. Similarly, the loading dock people can do a poor job of packing the truck. This means we have to make more deliveries."

Jim asked, "Would it make more sense to compute packing materials expense per box, per order, per pound, or as a percentage of revenue shipped?"

Susan responded, "Probably per box would be easiest."

Jim then inquired, "One problem with that measure is that it would further encourage the incomplete packing of boxes. Do you track pounds?"

"Yes," Susan said. "We have to because sometimes we are forced to use outside delivery services when we are backlogged. They charge by the pound."

"So the expenses your area affects are packing materials, truck expense, and outside vendor delivery expense?" Jim asked.

Job Position	Measure	Min	Max	Priority Weight
Plant Manager	Monthly Revenue	$400,000	$500,000	10%
	Scrap Expense / Revenue	17%	5%	10%
	Maintenance Expense / Pound	**$8.00**	**$6.00**	**15%**
	Labor Cost / Pound	$12.00	$9.00	20%
	DIO	60 days	40 days	5%
	6MMA # of Safety Incidents	1.5	.5	10%
	% Orders On Time	74%	100%	10%
	% Returns	7%	3%	10%
	% ISO 9000 Milestones Met	70%	100%	10%

Susan inquired, "What do you mean by truck expense—the cost of the trucks?"

Jim said, "No, it normally refers to fuel, maintenance, and fines."

"Then it makes sense," Susan agreed.

"For your scorecard, we could combine these three expenses and compare them to pounds shipped or revenue," Jim suggested.

"Yes, I think pounds would be a more valid measure since there is a mixed relationship between revenue and pounds," Susan said.

Jim replied, "Okay, we'll track the sum of the three expenses per pound. How many employees are there in your area?"

Shipping Mgr.	Monthly Revenue	$400,000	$500,000	10%
Susan	Pack+Truck+Vendor exp. / lb.	$2.10	$1.70	10%

Susan replied, "We have five packers, eight loaders, and ten drivers—a total of 23 employees."

Job Position	Measure	Min	Max	Priority Weight
Plant Manager	Monthly Revenue	$400,000	$500,000	10%
	Scrap Expense / Revenue	17%	5%	10%
	Maintenance Expense / Pound	$8.00	$6.00	15%
	Labor Cost / Pound	**$12.00**	**$9.00**	**20%**
	DIO	60 days	40 days	5%
	6MMA # of Safety Incidents	1.5	.5	10%
	% Orders On Time	74%	100%	10%
	% Returns	7%	3%	10%
	% ISO 9000 Milestones Met	70%	100%	10%

Jim reasoned, "Given that many employees, would you agree it makes sense to add a productivity measure to your scorecard?"

"That seems reasonable," Susan responded.

"What if we used the same denominator and tracked labor expense per pound delivered?" Jim recommended.

"Sounds good to me," Susan agreed.

"Sounds good to me too," Larry chimed in.

Shipping Mgr.	Monthly Revenue	$400,000	$500,000	10%
Susan	Pack+Truck+Vendor exp. / lb.	$2.10	$1.70	10%
	Shipping Labor Exp. / lb.	$6.10	$5.50	25%

Jim began again, "The next measure on Larry's scorecard is DIO which is *days inventory outstanding*. Does your area have any impact on inventory?"

Job Position	Measure	Min	Max	Priority Weight
Plant Manager	Monthly Revenue	$400,000	$500,000	10%
	Scrap Expense / Revenue	17%	5%	10%
	Maintenance Expense / Pound	$8.00	$6.00	15%
	Labor Cost / Pound	$12.00	$9.00	20%
	DIO	**60 days**	**40 days**	**5%**
	6MMA # of Safety Incidents	1.5	.5	10%
	% Orders On Time	74%	100%	10%
	% Returns	7%	3%	10%
	% ISO 9000 Milestones Met	70%	100%	10%

Susan responded, "Not really."

Larry began to get more involved in the process. "If your department doesn't get the orders out on time, ships incomplete orders, or orders are returned, then the materials are still in inventory."

Jim said, "That's true, Larry, but you are already measuring on-time shipments and returns under customer service. Won't that accomplish the same thing and be more understandable to the employees in the area?"

Larry replied, "Good point. We'll get at the issue with those measures."

"Okay, let's move on," Jim continued. "Larry's next measure is safety incidents. Can your employees have accidents?"

Job Position	Measure	Min	Max	Priority Weight
Plant Manager	Monthly Revenue	$400,000	$500,000	10%
	Scrap Expense / Revenue	17%	5%	10%
	Maintenance Expense / Pound	$8 00	$6.00	15%
	Labor Cost / Pound	$12.00	$9.00	20%
	DIO	60 days	40 days	5%
	6MMA # of Safety Incidents	**1.5**	**.5**	**10%**
	% Orders On Time	74%	100%	10%
	% Returns	7%	3%	10%
	% ISO 9000 Milestones Met	70%	100%	10%

"Oh, yes! All of them are at risk," Susan said.

"At the managerial level, we would usually measure the incidents for your area. However, when we get to the worker scorecards, I suggest you conduct a weekly, random safety audit and measure safe practices rather than incidents," Jim contended.

"Why's that?" Susan questioned.

Jim answered, "Because one way workers can reduce incidents is to simply not report them. Further, a prevention approach to safety is much preferable to simply counting recordable incidents."

"I see what you mean and it makes sense. Okay. Next!" Susan said.

Shipping Mgr	Monthly Revenue	$400,000	$500,000	10%
Susan	Pack+Truck+Vendor exp. / lb.	$2.10	$1.70	10%
	Shipping Labor Exp. / lb.	$6.10	$5.50	25%
	6MMA # of Safety Incidents	1.5	.5	15%

Jim began again, "The last two performance measures on Larry's scorecard are the percent orders returned and the percent orders on time. We'll only apply the ISO 9000 measure to people directly involved in the project. I'm pretty sure your people affect both on-time delivery and returns, don't they?"

Job Position	Measure	Min	Max	Priority Weight
Plant Manager	Monthly Revenue	$400,000	$500,000	10%
	Scrap Expense / Revenue	17%	5%	10%
	Maintenance Expense/ Pound	$8.00	$6.00	15%
	Labor Cost / Pound	$12.00	$9.00	20%
	DIO	60 days	40 days	5%
	6MMA # of Safety Incidents	1.5	.5	10%
	% Orders On Time	74%	100%	10%
	% Returns	7%	3%	10%
	% ISO 9000 Milestones Met	70%	100%	10%

Susan responded, "Yes, but when you say 'orders on time' do you mean with respect to our schedule or the customer's request? Sometimes their request dates are unrealistic; production can't produce the order due to a lack of inventory. Sometimes some of the drivers don't show up, sometimes the trucks break down, sometimes bad weather prevents making all the deliveries."

Jim replied, "If the customer doesn't get the order when expected, is he upset?"

Larry said, "You bet! I get a lot of the calls and our customers can't make their production schedules if we don't deliver their buttons on time."

Jim continued, "Do the customers really care why you missed the delivery date?"

"No," Larry and Susan said at the same time.

"Then the delivery date promised is what should be tracked," Jim argued. "Some of the factors that prevent delivery will become improvement initiatives later on."

Susan asked, "How are you going to track late deliveries that we were responsible for vs. mistakes in order entry, inventory control, or manufacturing?"

"Great question," Jim said with admiration. "In my opinion, when you have a linear process where the final outcome—on-time delivery of the correct order—depends on several areas, you should measure the final outcome and assign it to each area in the production-delivery chain."

Susan exclaimed, "You mean if production screws up, I get penalized!"

Jim responded, "Yes, but then again if your group makes an error, production is penalized. Measuring this way reduces finger-pointing and gets everyone to cooperatively seek solutions that will improve overall on-time, accurate deliveries. A lesser benefit is that if we tried to measure on-time and accurate performance for each group we would create a lot of internal, manual tracking. I agree that this approach violates the maximum group size of 10, but I believe the benefits outweigh the drawbacks."

Alice, the packing manager spoke up. "I agree with Jim that measuring all of us on the actual delivery performance is the best idea. It just might stop some of the arguing and get us to work together better!"

"What do you think, Susan?" Jim asked.

"I guess it might work," Susan said reluctantly.

Jim said, "Okay!" He then asked, "How would you priority weight your scorecard measures, Susan?"

Shipping Manager Performance Scorecard

Shipping Mgr.	Monthly Revenue	$400,000	$500,000	10%
Susan	Pack+Truck+Vendor exp. / lb.	$2.10	$1.70	10%
	Shipping Labor Exp. / lb.	$6.10	$5.50	25%
	6MMA # of Safety Incidents	1.5	.5	15%
	% Orders on Time	74%	100%	20%
	% Returns	7%	3%	20%

"What do you think of her priority weights Larry?" Jim asked.

"Well, Susan has put more emphasis on expense control and less on revenue which makes sense for her area. I like that 40 percent is assigned to quality measures. I think it's a great start!"

Jim announced, "I think that's enough for today. Tomorrow we'll get together with the three supervisors and Susan and design their scorecards. Then, the next day I'll work with the supervisors to design the worker scorecards. Do you have any questions?"

Tom, the loading supervisor, spoke up. "Shouldn't we have the workers involved in designing their own scorecards? That way we'll get better buy-in and ownership."

Jim responded "I've generally found it a good idea to design the first pass at the scorecards with the supervisors only. Giving the workers a blank sheet of paper rather than some sort of structure can backfire."

"So, they have no input in the design process?" Tom asked.

Jim said, "Sure they do. They will have an opportunity to modify the scorecards you present to them if it makes sense to management. We'll just start with a blueprint that will clarify for them what we are trying to accomplish."

For the next two weeks, Jim met with each area manager and their supervisors. The same procedure was used in each case. By the end of the month, everyone was assigned a scorecard with measures and priority weights. The final step of this phase was to assign preliminary min and max to each manager and supervisor's measures.

Summary of Management Scorecards Cascaded from the Plant Manager Scorecard

Job Position	Measure	Min	Max	Priority Weight
Plant Manager	Monthly Revenue	$400,000	$500,000	10%
Larry	Scrap Expense / Revenue	17%	5%	10%
	Maintenance Expense / 1000 units	$8.00	$6.00	15%
	Labor Cost / 1000 Units	$12.00	$9.00	20%
	DIO	60 days	40 days	5%
	6MMA # of Safety Incidents	1.5	.5	10%
	% Orders On Time	74%	100%	10%
	% Returns	7%	3%	10%
	% ISO 9000 Milestones Met	70%	100%	10%
Shipping Mgr.	Monthly Revenue	$400,000	$500,000	10%
Susan	Packing+Truck+Vendor exp. / lb.	$2.10	$1.70	10%
	Shipping Labor Exp. / 1000 units	$6.10	$5.50	25%
	6MMA # of Safety Incidents	1.5	.5	15%
	% Orders on Time	74%	100%	20%
	% Returns	7%	3%	20%
Loading Supervisor	Packing Expense / lb.	$0.60	$0.45	20%
Tom	Pounds / Loading Labor Hr.	.78	.50	25%
	Behavioral Safety Checklist %	80%	100%	15%
	% Orders on Time	74%	100%	20%
	% Returns	7%	3%	20%
Transportation Supervisor	Sales Referrals / Customer	0	.3	10%
Ed	Truck + Vendor Expense / lb.	$1.50	$1.20	10%
	Pounds / Transport Labor Hr.	$1.35	$1.00	25%
	Behavioral Safety Checklist %	80%	100%	15%
	% Orders on Time	74%	100%	20%
	% Returns	7%	3%	20%
Production Mgr	Scrap Expense / Revenue	17%	5%	15%
Alice	Maint. Expense / 1000 Units	$0.65	$0.40	5%
	Pounds / Production Labor Hr.	$1.21	$.90	25%
	Behavioral Safety Checklist %	80%	100%	15%
	% Orders on Time	74%	100%	20%
	% Returns	7%	3%	20%
Warehouse Mgr	Monthly Revenue	$400,000	$500,000	5%
Ahmed	Shrinkage %	2.25%	1.75%	5%
	Maintenance Expense / 1000 Units	$0.45	$0.35	10%
	Pounds / Warehouse Labor Hr.	$1.55	$1.10	20%
	DIO	60 days	40 days	15%
	6MMA # of Safety Incidents	80%	100%	15%
	% Orders On Time	74%	100%	15%
	% Returns	7%	3%	15%

Meeting to Design Scorecards for Workers

Susan, the shipping manager; Tom, the loading supervisor; and Jim, the consultant, met to further cascade Tom's performance measures to his subordinate workers.

Jim asked, "How many job positions report to you, Tom?"

Tom responded, "All six of my employees are loaders."

Loading Supervisor	Packing Expense / lb.	$0.60	$0.45	20%
Tom	Pounds / Loading Labor Hr.	.78	.50	25%
	Behavioral Safety Checklist %	80%	100%	15%
	% Orders on Time	74%	100%	20%
	% Returns	7%	3%	20%

Jim started, "We can design a performance scorecard for each individual loader, one scorecard for the entire loader team, or some combination of individual and team measures. The advantages of the individual scorecard are that a loader has more direct control over his scorecard results which is more motivating and fairer. The disadvantages of individual loader scorecards are they require a lot of data gathering and may discourage cooperation. What do you think Susan and Tom?"

Tom said, "They work together to load the trucks but some work harder than others. I'm afraid a team scorecard will be seen as unfair by the hard workers."

Jim responded, "Good point. We could measure them as a team except for productivity which we would measure individually. Or, we could add an attendance measure, or have the team members rate each member's contribution at the end of the month."

Susan said, "I like the individual attendance measure. Isn't the real problem that some loaders are absent a lot?"

Tom said, "You're right! Even so, when they are all here, some do more than others. But, if we could get everyone to show up, it would do a lot to improve our loading performance."

Jim replied, "Let's start with adding an attendance measure. If you still see a big difference in individual loader production, we can replace the attendance measure with individual productivity which reflects attendance as well." Here's what the loader team scorecard will look like:

Loading Team				
	Packing Expense / lb.	$0.60	$0.45	20%
	Pounds / Loading Labor Hr.	.78	.50	25%
	Behavioral Safety Checklist %	80%	100%	15%
	% Orders on Time	74%	100%	20%
	% Returns	7%	3%	20%
	Individual Attendance			

"How do you want to reweight the scorecard?"

Tom thought a minute and said, "Can we just move 10 percent from the team productivity measure to individual attendance? It occurs to me that the team will benefit from individuals being present since it will reduce their labor hours and increase the ratio. So the two measures are closely interrelated."

Jim responded, "Okay" and revised the chart. "Does this look good to you too, Susan?"

Susan said, "Yes, and I'm surprised at how easy this is, but I see why it was because we already had designed Tom's scorecard."

Loading Team				
	Packing Expense / lb.	$0.60	$0.45	20%
	Pounds / Loading Labor Hr.	.78	.50	15%
	Behavioral Safety Checklist %	80%	100%	15%
	% Orders on Time	74%	100%	20%
	% Returns	7%	3%	20%
	Individual Attendance	80%	100%	10%

Level I: Performance Scorecard System

Superior Button's Performance Scorecard System

Below are all of Superior Button's Performance Scorecards. The job position name, reporting relationship, and number of employees in the position are listed above each scorecard.

Company Strategic Scorecard (68 employees) (annual payroll = $2,720,000)

Measure	Min	Max	Priority Weight
Monthly Revenue	$400,000	$500,000	15%
Target Expenses / Revenue	18%	12%	20%
Labor Cost /Revenue	57%	35%	25%
DIO	60 days	40 days	10%
Total Monthly Incidents	1	0	10%
Account Attrition	18%	12%	10%
Project Milestones Met	70%	100%	10%

Chief Executive Officer (CEO) (1)

Measure	Min	Max	Priority Weight
Monthly Revenue	$400,000	$500,000	30%
Target Expense / Revenue	18%	12%	20%
Labor Cost / Revenue	57%	40%	30%
Account Attrition	18%	12%	20%

CEO's Administrative Assistant (reports to CEO) (1)

Measure	Min	Max	Priority Weight
CEO Performance Index	40%	100%	40%
Monthly Tasks Checklist %	80%	100%	40%
Average Phone Response Time	6 rings	3 rings	20%

Chief Financial Officer (CFO) (reports to CEO) (1)

Measure	Min	Max	Priority Weight
% Accurate Reports On Time	95%	100%	20%
% Average Budget Variance	12%	5%	25%
DIO	60 days	40 days	15%
% Accurate Billings	97%	100%	10%
% Vendor Payments On Time	87%	95%	10%
% Project Milestones Met	80%	100%	20%

Accounts Receivables Supervisor (reports to CFO) (1)

Measure	Min	Max	Priority Weight
% Accurate Reports On Time	85%	100%	20%
% Budget Variance	15%	0%	20%
Days Sales Outstanding	75 days	30 days	40%
% Charge-offs	6%	2%	20%

Accounts Receivables Clerk (reports to Accounts Receivables Supervisor) (2)

Measure	Min	Max	Priority Weight
Days Sales Outstanding	75 days	30 days	60%
% Charge-offs	6%	2%	40%

Order-Entry Supervisor (reports to CFO) (1)

Measure	Min	Max	Priority Weight
% Accurate Reports On Time	85%	100%	20%
% Budget Variance	15%	0%	20%
% Orders Entered Same Day	55%	100%	20%
% Accurate Orders	96%	100%	20%
Avg. Cust. Satisfaction Rating	2.4	4.0	20%

Order-Entry Clerk (reports to Order-Entry Supervisor) (3)

Measure	Min	Max	Priority Weight
% Orders Entered Same Day	55%	100%	30%
% Accurate Orders	96%	100%	30%
Avg. Cust. Satisfaction Rating	2.4	4.0	40%

Accounts Payable Clerk (reports to CFO) (2)

Measure	Min	Max	Priority Weight
% Vendor Payments On Time	87%	95%	40%
% Accurate Vendor Payments	95%	100%	40%
% Discounts Taken	50%	100%	20%

Purchasing/Inventory Manager (reports to CFO) (1)

Measure	Min	Max	Priority Weight
% Accurate Reports On Time	95%	100%	10%
Materials Cost / Revenue	23%	18%	20%
Scrap % Due to Materials	8%	2%	20%
% Runs Delay Due to Stock Out	14%	5%	30%
DIO	60 Days	40 Days	20%

Information Technology Officer (reports to CFO) (1)

Measure	Min	Max	Priority Weight
% Budget Variance	30%	0%	20%
% Uptime	96%	100%	30%
% Service Responses Same Day	35%	80%	50%

HR Director (reports to CEO) (1)

Measure	Min	Max	Priority Weight
Hiring Expense / Employee	$450	$300	20%
Days to Fill a Hire	40 days	20 days	20%
% New Hires Completing Probation	80%	90%	20%
6MMA # of Grievances	2.0	.5	10%
% Unforced Emp. Attrition	24%	15%	30%

Payroll/Benefits Clerk (reports to HR Director) (2)

Measure	Min	Max	Priority Weight
% Payrolls On Time	96%	100%	30%
% Payroll Accurate	98%	100%	30%
% Emp. Issues Resolved	50%	80%	40%

HR Representative (reports to HR Director) (1)

Measure	Min	Max	Priority Weight
% New Hires Completing Probation	80%	90%	25%
6MMA # of Grievances	2.0	.5	25%
% Unforced Emp. Attrition	24%	15%	15%
Emp. Orientations within 5 Days	50%	100%	15%
Training On Schedule	80%	100%	20%

Plant Manager (reports to CEO) (1)

Measure	Min	Max	Priority Weight
Monthly Revenue	$400,000	$500,000	10%
Scrap Expense / Revenue	17%	5%	10%
Maintenance Expense/1000 units	$8.00	$6.00	15%
Labor Cost / 1000 Units	$12.00	$9.00	20%
DIO	60 days	40 days	5%
6MMA # of Safety Incidents	1.5	.5	10%
% Orders On Time	74%	100%	10%
% Returns	7%	3%	10%
% ISO 9000 Milestones Met	70%	100%	10%

Warehouse Manager (reports to Plant Manager) (1)

Measure	Min	Max	Priority Weight
Monthly Revenue	$400,000	$500,000	5%
Shrinkage %	2.25%	1.75%	5%
Maintenance Expense / 1000 Units	$0.45	$0.35	10%
Pounds / Warehouse Labor Hr.	1. 55	2. 10	20%
DIO	60 days	40 days	15%
6MMA # of Safety Incidents	80%	100%	15%
% Orders On Time	74%	100%	15%
% Returns	7%	3%	15%

Warehouse Picker (reports to Warehouse Manager) (4)

Measure	Min	Max	Priority Weight
Picks / Labor Hour	35	55	30%
% Accurate Picks	78%	100%	30%
% Orders Delivered On Time	74%	100%	20%
% Order Returns	14%	5%	20%

Production Manager (reports to Plant Manager) (1)

Measure	Min	Max	Priority Weight
Scrap Expense / Revenue	17%	5%	15%
Maint. Expense / 1000 Units	$0.65	$0.40	5%
Pounds / Production Labor Hr.	1. 21	1. 85	25%
Behavioral Safety Checklist %	80%	100%	15%
% Orders on Time	74%	100%	20%
% Returns	7%	3%	20%

Production Cutting Supervisor (reports to Production Manager) (1)

Measure	Min	Max	Priority Weight
Scrap Expense / Revenue	17%	5%	15%
Maint. Expense / 1000 Units	$0.65	$0.40	5%
Pounds / Production Labor Hr.	1.65	2.40	25%
Behavioral Safety Checklist %	80%	100%	15%
% Orders on Time	74%	100%	20%
% Returns	7%	3%	20%

Production Cutter (reports to Cutting Supervisor) (8)

Measure	Min	Max	Priority Weight
Scrap Expense / Revenue	17%	5%	10%
Pounds / Production Labor Hr.	1.65	2.40	25%
Behavioral Safety Checklist %	80%	100%	25%
% Orders on Time	74%	100%	20%
% Returns	7%	3%	20%

Production-Finishing Supervisor (reports to Production Manager) (1)

Measure	Min	Max	Priority Weight
Scrap Expense / Revenue	17%	5%	15%
Maint. Expense / 1000 Units	$0.65	$0.40	5%
Pounds / Production Labor Hr.	1.21	1.85	25%
Behavioral Safety Checklist %	80%	100%	15%
% Orders on Time	74%	100%	20%
% Returns	7%	3%	20%

Production Finisher (reports to Finishing Supervisor) (7)

Measure	Min	Max	Priority Weight
Scrap Expense / Revenue	17%	5%	15%
Pounds / Production Labor Hr.	1.21	1.85	30%
Behavioral Safety Checklist %	80%	100%	15%
% Orders on Time	74%	100%	20%
% Returns	7%	3%	20%

Shipping and Receiving Manager (reports to Plant Manager) (1)

Measure	Min	Max	Priority Weight
Packing+Truck+Vendor exp. / lb.	$2.10	$1.70	10%
Shipping Labor Exp. / 1000 units	$6.10	$5. 50	25%
6MMA # of Safety Incidents	1. 5	. 5	15%
% Orders on Time	74%	100%	25%
% Returns	7%	3%	25%

Loading Supervisor (reports to Shipping and Receiving Manager) (1)

Measure	Min	Max	Priority Weight
Packing Expense / lb.	$0.60	$0.45	20%
Pounds / Loading Labor Hr.	.78	1.50	25%
Behavioral Safety Checklist %	80%	100%	15%
% Orders on Time	74%	100%	20%
% Returns	7%	3%	20%

Loaders (reports to Loading Supervisor) (5)

Measure	Min	Max	Priority Weight
Packing Expense / lb.	$0.60	$0.45	20%
Pounds / Loading Labor Hr.	.78	1.24	15%
Behavioral Safety Checklist %	80%	100%	15%
% Orders on Time	74%	100%	20%
% Returns	7%	3%	20%
Individual Attendance	80%	100%	10%

Inventory Stocker (reports to Shipping and Receiving Manager) (4)

Measure	Min	Max	Priority Weight
Picks / Labor Hour	35	55	30%
% Accurate Picks	78%	100%	30%
DIO	60 Days	40 Days	10%
% Runs Delay Due to Stock Out	14%	5%	30%

Transportation Supervisor (reports to Shipping and Receiving Manager)(1)

Measure	Min	Max	Priority Weight
Sales Referrals / Customer	0	.3	10%
Truck + Vendor Expense / lb.	$1.50	$1.20	10%
Pounds / Transport Labor Hr.	3.35	5.00	25%
Behavioral Safety Checklist %	80%	100%	15%
% Orders on Time	74%	100%	20%
% Returns	7%	3%	20%

Driver (reports to Transportation Supervisor) (5)

Measure	Min	Max	Priority Weight
Sales Referrals / Customer	0	.3	10%
Truck + Vendor Expense / lb.	$1.50	$1.20	10%
Pounds / Transport Labor Hr.	3.35	5.00	25%
Behavioral Safety Checklist %	80%	100%	15%
% Orders on Time	74%	100%	20%
% Returns	7%	3%	20%

Sales Manager (reports to CEO) (1)

Measure	Min	Max	Priority Weight
Monthly Revenue	$400,000	$500,000	50%
% Budget Variance	10%	0%	5%
Gross Margin %	18%	24%	20%
Sales Labor / Revenue	14%	12%	5%
DIO	60 days	40 days	5%
Account Attrition %	18%	12%	15%

Marketing Assistant (reports to Sales Manager) (1)

Measure	Min	Max	Priority Weight
% Marketing Projects On Time	85%	100%	30%
% Budget Variance	10%	0%	10%
% New Accounts Added	1%	5%	60%

Salesperson (reports to Sales Manager) (6)

Measure	Min	Max	Priority Weight
% Monthly Revenue Goal	70%	100%	60%
Gross Margin %	18%	24%	20%
DIO	60 days	40 days	10%
Account Attrition %	18%	12%	10%

Quality Assurance Manager (reports to Plant Manager) (1)

Measure	Min	Max	Priority Weight
Target Expense / Revenue	18%	12%	10%
Labor Cost / Revenue	57%	35%	30%
DIO	60 days	40 days	10%
Total Recordables	1	0	20%
ISO 9000 Milestones Met	70%	100%	30%

These performance scorecards will be referred to, and in some cases modified, throughout the remaining chapters.

Chapter 17

Level I: Performance System Manager and Facilitator Roles

Jim met with Julie (the HR director and new performance system manager) and Juanita (the quality control manager and new facilitator).

Jim started, "Julie, you have been assigned as the performance system manager for Superior Button. Juanita, your new role is that of a facilitator." Jim went to the whiteboard and wrote the following list. "These are the duties of the performance system manager," he said.

1. Create a policies and procedures manual.
2. Train managers in the components of the performance system.
3. Present employee orientations and distribute employee-orientation handouts.
4. Provide ongoing communications.
5. Ensure timely and accurate reporting and incentive pay.
6. Conduct system reviews.
7. Create and complete a transition plan.

Jim continued, "Julie, you will need to prepare a policies and procedure manual for the organization."

1. Create a policies and procedures manual.

"What items should be included?" Julie asked.

Jim replied, "Similar to your human resources manual, you should state who is eligible to participate in the system and under what conditions they are not. When do new employees begin to participate? Very important is how often will scorecard measures, priority weights, mins or maxes be reviewed and possibly changed? What will be the criteria and who will decide? You will need to prepare reporting and performance payout procedures including who reports and by when. What penalties will be applied for late or inaccurate data reporting? What actions will be taken when an employee consistently falls short of minimally acceptable performance?"

"When should the manual be ready?" Julie asked.

"Before the first month of profit-indexed performance pay," Jim responded.

2. Train managers in the components of the performance system.

Jim stated, "We have already trained the managers in basic performance coaching skills and you worked with them one-on-one to improve their skills. In addition, you should provide a short workshop on scorecard features, how the performance index is computed, and how profit-indexed performance pay will be computed."

3. Present employee orientations and distribute employee-orientation handouts.

Julie asked, "What should be included in the orientations and handouts?"

Jim continued, "Three key employee concerns are 1) Will the scorecard scores be used punitively? 2) Are the scorecard measures, mins, and maxes reasonable? 3) How will my performance pay be calculated? I suggest that in the orientation sessions you give employees sample data and let them compute the scorecard performance index and payout. I would continue the orientation session until everyone could compute both."

4. Provide ongoing communications.

Jim said, "Each week you should meet with managers who are having difficulties as identified by the performance scorecards. You should also meet with managers who are demonstrating success and recognize their success. With regard to recognition, you might want to consider a quarterly performance newsletter in which max-level performances or improvements are recognized. However, make sure your recognition is never seen as a competition. You should also meet monthly with the executive group to summarize the systems successes and failures."

5. Ensure timely and accurate reporting and incentive pay.

Julie said with concern, "I understand timely reporting and incentive pay, but I'm not sure how I will know if reporting is accurate."

Jim remarked, "First, if the system is truly based on positive reinforcement rather than punishment, there will be considerably less cheating. Reported data that falls outside the min or max suggests inaccurate data may have been reported. Perfectly consistent data across months suggests that the person reporting the data is possibly inventing it. Extreme differences across employees on a measure may also indicate inaccurate reporting. Inaccurate reporting typically can only occur with manually collected data, which limits the items you need to be concerned with. In the unusual circumstance that you suspect a systemic problem, you might implement random audits of the reported data."

6. Conduct system reviews.

"What do you mean by a system review?" Julie inquired.

Jim replied, "I suggest you conduct a total performance system review every six months for the first year or two of system implementation and then annually thereafter. The review is presented to the senior management group and Juanita, the facilitator. We'll discuss the specifics of such a review at a later date when we have actual data. The audit will review the validity of the scorecard and performance pay components. Sid, the planner, will describe changes in the metasystem such as competition, technology, resources, regulations, customer needs, and economic conditions. A discussion will follow as to what changes to the performance system best address these issues."

7. Create and complete a transition plan.

Jim sat down and said, "Finally, you will be responsible for creating and achieving a transition plan."

Julie looked deeply puzzled and asked "What do you mean by a transition plan? A transition to what?"

Jim laughed and said, "Remember Sid wants to move Superior Button to a self-managed workplace. As I described in our first workshop, there are typically four levels that must be transitioned through to achieve this goal. We are in the first level which is implementing performance measurement and positive leadership as well as removing performance constraints. The first two tasks are yours, Julie, and the third is Juanita's."

For the first time Juanita spoke, "Okay, what are the other levels and when do we implement them?"

Jim responded, "The transition to each level is not determined by the passage of time but by the effectiveness and success of each level. Some organizations never reach the second or later levels, but these are not failures since each level provides its own benefits to the organization and its employees. Once we are successful with Level I, the transition to Level II is natural. That is, once employees are convinced the measures, mins, and maxes are reasonable, that managers will assist them in achieving them, and that most constraints to achieving the maxes are removed, many will be receptive to Stakeholder Pay, in which an increased performance pay opportunity is substituted for some or all of guaranteed base pay. Employees will be willing to take a reasonable stake in company profits if they are confident their share will be fairly and consistently distributed."

Julie asked, "So what types of incentives are provided in Level I?"

Jim answered, "Juanita will manage a performance improvement project initiative in Level I that provides one-time cash awards to individuals or teams for meeting target improvements on selected scorecard measures. Juanita will be trained in performance analysis and improvement and then assist the managers in designing and implementing their improvement projects."

Jim continued, "In the first phase of Level II, Profit-Indexed Performance Pay will be implemented in place of an annual, base-pay increase. The performance pay opportunity will be three times that of the withheld base-pay increase. For example, if profits, inflation, or competition indicate the need for a 3 percent, base-pay increase, a 9 percent performance pay opportunity will be provided in its place."

"I see my role now as the facilitator," Juanita said enthusiastically. "I will be managing the performance improvement program, helping managers pinpoint scorecard-improvement opportunities, and then designing and implementing performance improvement projects. But what about after that?"

"Performance improvement is a continuous process and will not stop simply because we move to Level II," Jim answered. "In fact, as employees become stakeholders, your services will be even more valuable. In addition, you both will have a lot of involvement in Levels III and IV."

"Tell us what those are again?" Juanita asked.

Jim answered, "Level III is concerned with job enrichment. When employees become stakeholders they will need to, and want to,

expand their job skills, take on more decision-making, and optimize their work schedules in order to consistently earn high levels of performance pay."

Julie asked, "Can you give us some examples of job enrichment?"

"Sure," Jim replied. Jim's examples included the following:

1. *Job enlargement*—Job functions are expanded to reduce the number of unique job positions.

2. *Job enrichment*—Decision-making authority for selected processes is transferred from the manager to the subordinate.

3. *Flexible scheduling*—Employees agree to part-time work arrival and departure times based upon input volume cycles.

4. *Work prospecting*—During low, work-input periods, additional work is brought into the department from other areas or outside the organization.

5. *Cross-utilization*—during low, work-input periods, employees work in areas outside the department. This strategy involves cross-training employees.

"And Julie and I will be assigned to make these happen?" Juanita wondered.

Jim said, "That's correct. You two, the managers, and the workers will develop and implement these job enrichment strategies. When they have been successfully implemented, the company will be in a position to move to the final level, Level IV: Self-Managed Teams, if you so choose."

Jim continued, "In Level IV, we will turn over most decision-making authority to individual workers or worker teams. The manager span of control will be increased and manager performance pay opportunity will increase as they take on more subordinates without a decline in scorecard performance."

Julie exclaimed, "Sounds pretty organized but really challenging. We're ready to get going!"

Chapter 18

Level I: Improving Management Practices

A performance measurement test run was conducted in January by Julie, the new performance system manager. She first gave a brief orientation to the managers and supervisors regarding the purposes of the system and what data, if any, each manager or supervisor was to collect during or at the end of the month. Julie worked with the programmer and Superior Button's management information system to export measurement data to the new performance system database. For new measures, where data were unavailable, Julie and the programmer developed screen-capture forms for the managers and supervisors to use to enter data.

In February, Julie imported the January data to the new performance system database (PSD) and processed the scorecards. Missing or inaccurate data were identified and corrective actions taken. The scorecards measures were then examined for data that fell outside the measures' min-max ranges. The project team met and reviewed these outlier measures and adjusted the min and/or max accordingly. It was decided that a second test-run month would be prudent and data were collected for the month of February. In March, the second month's results were reviewed and the project team decided the data and scorecards were acceptable.

Julie then administered a management practices survey to all employees. Each employee rated the manager or supervisor to whom they reported. These ratings were then compared to each employee's

February scorecard performance score. The scores were then plotted on the leadership matrix.

The management practices survey was administered after the first full month of reporting. The survey was administered to identify managers that were not practicing positive management skills. This identification was critical to the success of the measurement system since there would likely be some managers who used the new performance scorecards as an aversive instrument by focusing on and criticizing poor performance on the scorecard. If these aversive practices were not identified and corrected, the scorecards would have failed to function as a positive reinforcement system.

The following is a sample leadership matrix which compares each manager's average management-practices rating on the above survey to their subordinates' average scorecard performance index. A perfect score would be plotted in the upper right-hand corner. That is, the manager received a perfect rating on their management practices and their subordinates all performed at max on their performance scorecards.

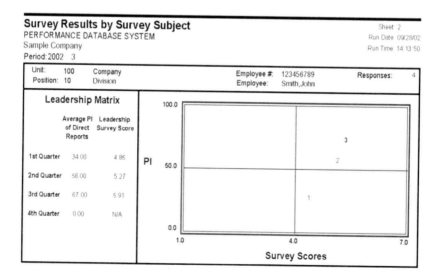

Managers who fall in the lower left quadrant are not likely to really be managing since their subordinates are performing poorly and have rated their management practices as poor. These managers are termed *absentee managers*. Managers that fall in the lower right quadrant are rated well by their subordinates but their subordinates perform poorly. These managers are well liked by employees but fail to focus on employee performance. These managers are termed *paternalistic managers*.

Managers who fall in the upper left quadrant obtain high subordinate performance, but likely do so using aversive techniques such as criticism and threats. These managers are referred to as *autocratic managers*. Finally, the upper-right hand quadrant managers are termed *positive leadership* in that they secure high employee performance using positive management techniques. Employing these techniques is critical to the success of the Level I transition to the liberated workplace.

Jim and Julie met to review the 15 managers. The survey and employee scorecard results were plotted on the leadership matrix. The results are below.

Absentee Managers	3
Paternalistic Managers	5
Autocratic Managers	4
Positive Leadership	3
	15

Jim looked up from the survey results of the 15 managers and supervisors and said, "Management in your organization appears to be a major problem! Only three of the 15 managers fall in the positive leadership quadrant of your leadership matrix."

Julie responded, "Many of our managers were promoted from within. They have never had any formal management training or any review of their management techniques."

Jim, surprised, responded, "I would be pleased to offer a one-day workshop on positive leadership if you wish. I've conducted many of them at the bank."

Julie, delighted, declared, "That would be great! I've tried to talk Sid into offering management training ever since I got here."

Jim and Julie decided that Jim should conduct a positive leadership workshop for the managers. Following the workshop, Julie would meet individually with the managers, review their survey and matrix results, and observe their management techniques to provide personal coaching.

Several days later, Jim began the manager workshop. "Welcome," he announced. "It's great to meet all of you and share some ideas that will make it easier to work with your employees. The workshop will last till four with a couple of breaks and a break for lunch. Any questions before we get started?"

No one asked any questions.

"Fine," Jim said hesitantly. "Let me start by asking you if all your employees perform equally?"

Martina, the shipping and receiving manager spoke up, "Obviously, some employees perform better than others."

Jim asked, "Why don't all employees perform well?"

Larry, the plant manager, frowned and said, "Some employees just have a bad attitude."

Jim wrote on the whiteboard, BAD ATTITUDE. "Any other reasons?" he asked.

Elaine, the sales manager, put her hand up and said, "Some people are just lazy!"

Jim wrote LAZY. "Any other reasons for poor performance?" asked Jim.

Margaret, the CFO, said haughtily, "Some people are just dumb!"

Jim wrote DUMB on the whiteboard.

The whiteboard now listed three descriptions:

BAD ATTITUDE

LAZY

DUMB

Jim then said, "These are three explanations for poor performance. How do we know if an employee has a bad attitude, is lazy, or is dumb?"

"You can tell," said Arthur, the warehouse manager. "They make a lot of mistakes and don't get things done on time."

Jim responded, "So, employees with these issues don't perform well and we know they have these issues because they don't perform well."

Arthur said, "Wait a minute! That's circular reasoning isn't it?"

Jim asserted, "Yes it is. We often explain why people don't perform well by referring to internal states or traits like attitude, laziness or lack of intelligence. These internal states are not directly observable, but only inferred from the person's behavior. So they really aren't explanations at all. And, even if they were, there isn't much a manager can do about them."

Bert, the IT guy, exclaimed, "So what you are saying is that if we want to understand someone's performance, we need to look at their situation for the causes instead of inside them."

"Perfect," Jim declared. "That is exactly what I am saying. Can anyone give me some examples of factors in the work environment that might affect an employee's performance?"

Julie, the HR Director and new PSM spoke up, "Well, in HR we look at their prior education and work experiences when we are considering hiring someone."

"Right," Jim responded, "But what are the environmental factors in the current workplace that might affect performance?"

Emily, the order-entry supervisor, said quietly, "How other employees treat them and how they are supervised affects people's performances."

"Now we're on to something," Jim observed. "The people in this room may or may not be able to affect the way other employees treat someone, but they certainly can affect how they are supervised."

"Okay, I see that," Larry remarked. "But everything isn't just about how we get along with our subordinates. As Julie said, their background and training as well as tools, supplies, and many other things affect how well they perform."

Jim walked to the whiteboard and posted the following:

PERFORMANCE CONSTRAINTS

OPPORTUNITY   CAPABILITY   CONTEXT

Jim spoke, "Some environmental factors affect an employee's opportunity to perform, like the volume of work, work schedules, and work distribution. We call these *opportunity constraints*. Other factors affect an employee's capability to perform. Julie mentioned two of these—experience and training. Larry also pointed out others like tools and supplies. We call these *capability constraints*. Finally, the way a person is managed affects their performance. We call these *context constraints*. Today we'll focus on context constraints. In a few weeks we'll have a second workshop that focuses on opportunity and capability constraints. "Let's take a break, and when we get back, I'll talk about the components of work context and management."

After the break, everyone sat down and Jim started, "So we've talked about not blaming employees or unseen internal states for poor performance, but rather the workplace environment. We discussed the three categories of workplace environment performance constraints. We'll discuss context or management constraints today and the other two at a later time," said Jim. He wrote on the whiteboard:

ABC's of Performance

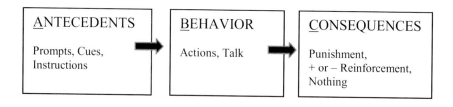

ANTECEDENTS	BEHAVIOR	CONSEQUENCES
Prompts, Cues, Instructions	Actions, Talk	Punishment, + or − Reinforcement, Nothing

Jim started, "You can think of context in terms of an ABC Model in which **B** stands for an employee's behavior. Antecedents come right before the behavior and Consequences right after. Antecedents prompt and guide a behavior and the behavior's consequences determine how often the behavior will occur."

Jim continued, "Examples of antecedents include prompts, cues, instructions, guides, requests, complaints, and so forth. To be optimally effective, prompts should be immediate, specific, and predictive." Jim wrote on the whiteboard:

Immediate—to prompt a behavior, an antecedent should occur as soon as possible before the behavior is to occur.

Specific—an effective antecedent informs the employee as to the behaviors: who, what, when, and where.

Predictive—antecedents should predict a consequence for the behavior—the why.

Jim turned to the group and inquired, "Any questions or comments?"

Arthur, the warehouse manager, asked, "I understand immediate and specific, but don't follow what you mean by *predictive*."

Jim replied, "*Predictive* means that the prompt carries with it the assurance of a successful outcome for the performer. In a sense, it is the credibility of the prompt for the performer. For example, say your parents told you to clean up your room or else you won't get dinner. But they never follow through and you always get dinner. Then the prompt, 'clean up your room' implies no consequence for the behavior and you may choose not to comply."

Jim continued, "Or, I might tell you the best way to wrap a package, but my instructions in the past have proven ineffective or incorrect. In this case, you might ignore my prompt. Prompts have to predict successful behavior and consequences. They have to be credible and the source has to be credible."

"I see," Arthur responded.

Jim then said, "Let me give you some examples and you tell me if they are effective prompts or not. The first one is this: 'We need to get the work out soon!'"

Susan, the production manager, asserted, "That violates all the rules. It's not timely, specific, or predictive. 'Soon' doesn't say exactly when, 'work' doesn't say what, and the consequences of getting it out are not specified."

"Excellent," Jim beamed. "How about, 'We need to get the work out by this Wednesday.'"

Elaine, the sales manager, responded, "It tells you when but not what or why."

"Very good," Jim said. "Then what about, 'We need to get the Johnson order out by this Wednesday.'"

"Better," Emily declared, "But still doesn't say who or why."

"Okay," Jim replied, "Let's try, 'Martha, Bob, and Terry need to get the Johnson work order out by Wednesday to get our payment on time.'"

"Good," Julie stated, "But it could be a little better if the exact time on Wednesday was stated."

"I think you've got it," Jim asserted in his best Henry Higgins voice. "Let's move on from A to C—consequences. Consequences include feedback, reinforcement, punishment, or nothing. Let's begin by discussing what the main differences are between work and play. Give me some examples of play."

Several managers spoke up and the list included hobbies, games, and sports. "What makes these activities play?" Jim asked.

Martina, the shipping and receiving manager, responded, "They are fun!"

"Okay, Jim replied, "but what makes them fun?"

Everyone sat quietly with puzzled looks on their faces. After a while Jim said, "What makes them fun is that they contain immediate feedback and consequences. Who wants to tell us what their favorite hobby, game, or sport is?" he asked.

"I like to play tennis," Sid stated.

"Does tennis have immediate feedback?" Jim asked.

Sid replied, "Yes, if you hit the ball right you score, and you don't score if you hit it wrong."

Jim then said, "What about consequences?"

Sid responded, "If you hit it wrong often enough, you lose the game."

Jim continued, "If you think about it, most play has built-in feedback and consequences. But what about work? How often and how immediately does good performance receive recognition and reinforcement?"

Sid said, "Well I guess annual reviews and salary increases aren't very often and certainly not very immediate. How could we change that?"

Jim commented, "It is possible to purchase or program immediate feedback for employees who work at computers. Pop-up screens or files can be used to provide such feedback. However, many tasks do not involve computers, at least in real time. In some cases the employee can keep their own log or chart of behavior. The most controllable feedback by you is to provide the feedback in person or use memos, e-mail, or wall posters. For a manager to provide effective feedback, he must observe employees doing something right—not just their mistakes. Feedback for mistakes tells us what not to do, but not necessarily what to do. How many of you make a positive comment on a regular basis when an employee meets a deadline, handles a difficult customer, or solves a problem?"

Eight of the 15 managers raised their hands—exactly the number that received good management practices survey results.

"Julie will work with those of you who haven't developed this skill," Jim declared. "You have to know when an effective behavior or improvement occurs and then know what to say. There are three other characteristics of good feedback in addition to immediacy and frequency. These are goals, trend charts, and linked consequences. Goals tell us when performance is good. Most hobbies, games, and sports have goals within them. Charts tell us about performance trends over time. Are we getting better or worse?" Jim went to the whiteboard and drew a chart.

Jim continued, "On day one the employee sees he is not at goal. On days two and three he sees that he is improving. On day four he knows he has met goal. The chart gives a sense of progress and the goal an objective for the employee that one-time recognition does not. Employees can keep their own charts, anonymous data can be posted on a wall chart with I. D. numbers, charts can be e-mailed to the employee, or a file or website provided where the employees can find their charts.

"Finally," Jim remarked, "Introducing feedback typically improves employee performance immediately. However, to sustain the effects of feedback, the feedback has to relate to consequences. Consistently telling an employee they did a good job begins to lose its effect on performance if nothing of personal benefit results. It's like the ad, 'Where's the beef?'"

Jim continued, "We have talked about prompts and feedback, but not about consequences. As I've said, both prompts and feedback must ultimately relate to consequences to maintain their effectiveness. Behaviorists categorize consequences as positive reinforcement, negative reinforcement, positive punishment, and negative punishment. I'll list these concepts on the board."

Positive Reinforcement	Increases behavior by adding something desirable
Negative Reinforcement	Increases behavior by removing something undesirable
Positive Punishment	Decreases behavior by adding something undesirable
Negative Punishment	Decreases behavior by removing something desirable

Jim asked, "When a manager says, 'Get this done by closing or you will be fired!' what type of consequence is he using?"

Larry spoke up, "He's using positive punishment!"

Jim responded, "Does everyone agree with Larry?" Everyone nodded their heads in agreement. "Well, is the manager making this threat to get the employee to do something or stop doing something?" Jim asked.

Several people said simultaneously, "They are trying to get them to finish the job by closing!"

Jim replied, "But punishment decreases behavior rather than increases it. It is a common confusion to think that all unpleasant or aversive events are necessarily punishment. In fact, in business organizations employees are much more often threatened to get work done, not to stop a behavior. For example, is a salary a positive reinforcer or a negative reinforcer? That is, does the salaried employee work during the month to get the check or to avoid losing it? Similarly, does the employee work for the supervisor to gain recognition or to avoid criticism?"

The room was silent. Jim could tell that everyone was thinking this question through. Finally, Larry spoke. "I think most of us believe people work to earn their checks, not to avoid losing them. We also think that employees work to gain supervisor approval, not to avoid their criticism. But, as I think it through, there probably are a lot of employees who work to avoid being demoted or fired and to avoid supervisor criticism and bad performance reviews."

Jim said, "Let's follow this logic. If an employee goofs off most of the time, what happens to her?"

"If she is caught goofing off, she will be criticized by the supervisor, may get a poor review, and ultimately might get demoted or fired," stated Susan emphatically.

Jim continued, "If an employee produces twice as much as others, what happens to her?"

Susan continued, "She may get a compliment from the supervisor, a good review, and a salary increase or promotion."

Jim stated, "Susan's first set of consequences are defined as negative reinforcement. Her second set of consequences are defined as positive reinforcement. We are going to change the pay system from straight salary to a salary plus monthly pay for performance. This will shift employee pay from mostly negative reinforcement to a mix of negative and positive reinforcement.

"According to the management practices survey we conducted last month, about half of the managers use recognition of good or improved performance to manage employees. This is positive reinforcement. However, the other half uses threats and criticism, which is negative reinforcement. Julie will work with you to help you implement the use of positive reinforcement in your management. Although, some managers do get results through intimidation, we are trying to change our organizational culture to one that relies more on positive than negative reinforcement. We believe that this transition will reduce employee absenteeism and turnover, improve morale and cooperation, and ultimately improve employee performance.

"Thank you for your time. We look forward to working with you to make Superior Button a highly successful organization and a great place to work. Julie will be contacting you to set up a coaching visit."

Julie reviewed the leadership matrix and found that all four of the autocratic managers were in the plant. These included the plant manager, Larry; the production manager, Susan; the production-cutting supervisor, Nikita; and the finishing supervisor, Denny.

Jim had told Julie that it was common for middle and line managers to model the management style of their superiors. In these cases, the best practice was to begin the coaching sessions with the senior manager and work down. Further, the fact that only the production area was managed autocratically suggested that the likely problem interaction was between the plant manager and the production manager. Julie met with both managers to observe their styles of interacting with each other. It required three sessions to work out the issues and move the relationship to a positive one.

Chapter 19

Level I: Performance Improvement Projects

A performance improvement program was designed by Juanita and Jim after the performance scorecards had been successfully reported for three months. The three months of data provided Juanita and the managers a minimal performance trend for each measure to assist in pinpointing measures to be targeted for performance improvement projects.

Juanita held a meeting with the managers to explain the program. She began, "Thanks for coming. As you may know, I've been assigned to be the new facilitator for the company. My job is to manage our performance improvement program that begins next month. Each manager will select one measure from his scorecard, or his reports' scorecards, and implement a performance improvement project to improve performance on the targeted measure. If a 30 percent or greater improvement in the measure is achieved within 90 days, the manager and his reports will all receive a $100 check for their efforts."

One of the managers inquired, "What if we don't achieve a 30 percent improvement in 30 days? That seems pretty ambitious!"

Juanita answered, "Research finds that a 30 percent improvement is the average improvement. That's why we selected it as a target. If you don't achieve the goal, you will still benefit from the improvement in how well your area functions. You can also implement a different improvement strategy to get to the 30 percent or select another measure.

"Are there other questions before I get started?" Juanita asked. There were none. "Let's start by discussing the typical steps in an improvement project," she said. Juanita went to the whiteboard and wrote the following steps:

1. Select improvement target from scorecard
2. Define critical behaviors as needed
3. Pinpoint performance constraints
4. Design or select performance improvement plan
5. Conduct cost-benefit analysis

Juanita turned to the group and said "We'll begin with selecting a performance improvement target. In each scorecard assigned to you, you will be looking for the measure that displays the most performance improvement potential (PIP). Our analysis will look at performance trends. That is, how performance changes over time."

"Five trend conditions indicate a measure's PIP," she explained. Juanita drew five charts on the whiteboard. After she had drawn the five trend conditions she said, "The first condition is when the measure data is flat and consistently well below the max. The distance between the average performance across time and the max is the PIP. However, this PIP is speculative since max performance has never actually been achieved.

"The second situation is a declining trend. The PIP is the distance between the current performance and the previous high performance. The third PIP is presented by data that is highly variable or cyclic. This PIP is the distance between the lowest and highest performances. The fourth PIP can only be computed if the measure data is tracked for individual performers. The PIP is the distance between the exemplar performer and the average performer. The final PIP is based on data that over time has become more variable. The PIP is the distance between the worst current performance and the original stable performance."

"Which PIP is likely to yield the most or quickest improvement?" Denny, a supervisor, asked.

Juanita responded, "Good question. This will depend on the type of constraint that is holding back performance. Some constraints are relatively easy to remove while others require a lot of effort. I suggest you pick two or three measures that demonstrate high PIPs. Later, when you determine their constraints, you can select the one that yields the highest cost-benefit."

Five Types of PIP's

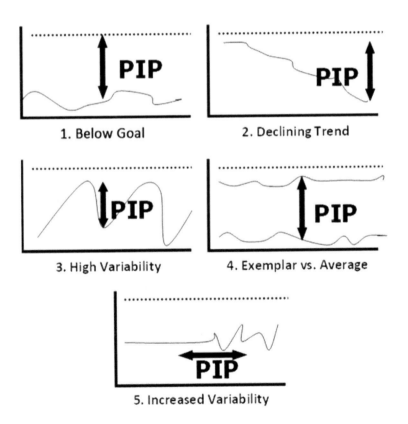

1. Below Goal

2. Declining Trend

3. High Variability

4. Exemplar vs. Average

5. Increased Variability

"Let's move on to step two in your performance improvement project: define behaviors. In some cases, you may want to identify and track a sub-result or behavior that you believe drives the scorecard measure. For example, if the scorecard measure is total sales, you might want to target prospecting, closing, cross-sell, or up-sell as a means of improving total sales. If the scorecard measure is productivity you might want to track efficiency, utilization, or rework. In most cases, however, the scorecard measures were selected because they were actionable for employees and you will track them directly. Any questions?"

"I'm not sure what sub-results or behaviors you are talking about!" Emily exclaimed.

Juanita smiled and replied, "Don't worry. I'll be working with you and I have had a good deal of training in identifying the drivers of final results. That ends class for today. What I would like each of you to do, over the next three days, is to review your scorecard charts and select three potential target measures for your performance improvement project. If you want help on analyzing PIPs or defining sub-results or behaviors, call me and I'll come by and work with you. Any questions?"

Juanita continued, "Let's practice targeting measures for improvement projects. Who is willing to share their scorecard charts?" Emily, the order-entry supervisor, and Elaine, the sales manager, raised their hands.

"Would you go down the hall and make copies for every one of the scorecard and the measure charts you want to work on? We'll take a short break in the meantime," said Juanita.

When everyone returned, they each received copies of two scorecards and seven trend charts.

Order Entry Clerk (reports to Order Entry Supervisor) (3 employees)

Measure	Min	Max	Priority Weight
% Orders Entered Same Day	55%	100%	30%
% Accurate Orders	96%	100%	30%
Avg. Cust. Satisfaction Rating	2. 4	4. 0	40%

Salesperson (reports to Sales Manager) (6)

Measure	Min	Max	Priority Weight
% Monthly Revenue Goal	70%	100%	60%
Gross Margin %	18%	24%	20%
DIO	60 days	40 days	10%
Account Attrition %	18%	12%	10%

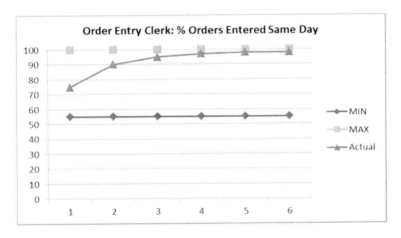

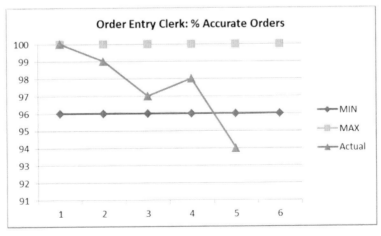

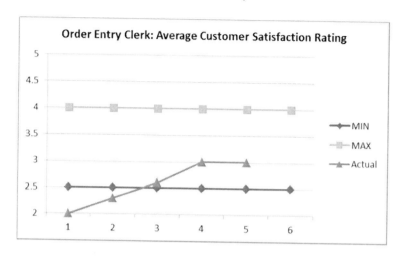

"Emily, which measure on your employees' scorecard has the greatest performance improvement potential?" Juanita asked.

"Well, it's obvious that order accuracy is getting worse and the other two measures are improving. I'd target order accuracy for my project," Emily answered.

"Good," Juanita agreed. "Let's look at Elaine's salespeople's performance. Which measure would you target, Elaine?"

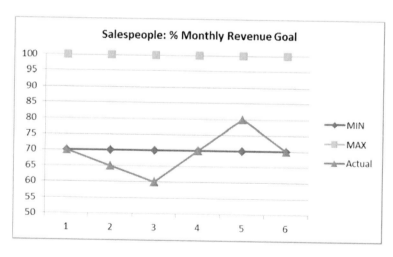

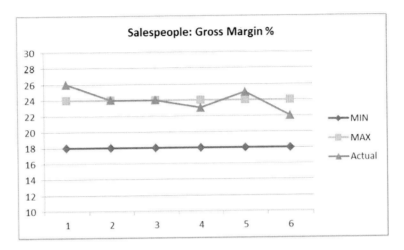

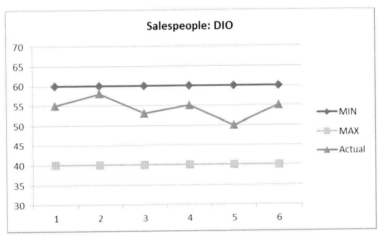

Elaine replied, "DIO is at max but all three of the others could stand improvement. However, the one that would have the most impact, and is furthest from goal, is the measure meeting the monthly revenue goals. I'd target that one."

Juanita summarized, "Okay, we've selected our target measures. Emily will target percent accurate orders and Elaine will target the percent monthly revenue goal met. Now we move on to the second step in a performance improvement project—defining critical behaviors.

1. Select improvement target from scorecard
2. Define critical behaviors as needed
3. Pinpoint performance constraints
4. Design or select performance improvement plan
5. Conduct cost-benefit analysis

"Emily, is the measure *percent accurate orders* actionable or do we need to break it down to specific behaviors?" Juanita asked.

Emily thought a minute and said, "It seems like a good measure as it is."

"Good!" Juanita agreed. "Elaine, how about percent revenue goal met?"

"There are a lot steps that go into making a sale," Elaine responded.

Juanita replied, "That's true and a number of different behaviors." She went to the board and drew the following table.

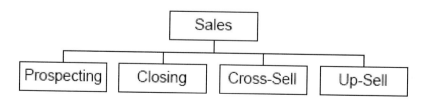

Juanita turned and said, "All these behaviors affect sales. Is there one in particular that you think is a high opportunity?"

Elaine said enthusiastically, "Definitely. My salespeople need to improve on prospecting. They just visit the customers they are comfortable with and miss a lot of opportunities."

"Great," Juanita exclaimed. "Emily's target will be percent accurate orders and Elaine's will be prospecting. We'll define prospecting as number of approved prospects called upon. That way, they won't call on their grandmother and count it as a prospect." Everyone laughed and the workshop ended for the day.

1. Select improvement target from scorecard
2. Define critical behaviors as needed
3. Pinpoint performance constraints
4. Design or select performance improvement plan
5. Conduct cost-benefit analysis

When the group reconvened the following day, Juanita said, "Now that we have selected our target order-entry scorecard measure, and sales behavior of prospecting, we are ready to figure out what constraint is causing each PIP." Juanita went to the whiteboard and drew the following table:

Performance Improvement Plans

1. Select improvement target from scorecard
2. Define critical behaviors as needed
3. Pinpoint performance constraints
4. Design or select performance improvement plan
5. Conduct cost-benefit analysis

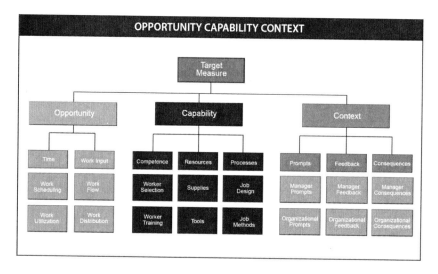

"There are three primary constraints that impede performance," Juanita stated. "These are listed at the top of the constraint analysis table and are opportunity constraints, capability constraints, and context constraints. The first step in your constraint analysis is to identify which primary constraint is most responsible for holding back your employees' performance.

"I have passed out some sheets that list questions you should ask yourselves to determine the type of constraint that is producing poor performance. Emily and Elaine, read through the lists and tell me if any seem relevant to your employees. If any of the questions don't make sense, stop and ask me to clarify."

Emily and Elaine read through the decision-tree lists.

Time Constraints

Are employees provided sufficient time to complete their tasks?

If no, then work scheduling and/or worker utilization are the likely constraints.

Is there work left undone at the end of the day?
If yes, there may be an under-scheduling constraint.

Is there enough work to fill each employee's typical day?
If no, the area has an over-scheduling constraint.

Are employees regularly assigned other tasks such as training, meetings, and special projects?
If yes, you may have a work-utilization constraint.

Do absences conform to company policy?
If no, you may have an absenteeism constraint.

Work-Input Constraints
Is there sufficient and consistent work input?
If no, then workflow may be the constraint.

Is work returned by your unit to a sending or upstream unit?
If yes, than your unit may have a workflow constraint.

Is the upstream unit's work arrival often late?
If yes, than your unit may have a workflow constraint.

Is work input cyclical during the day, week, month, or season?
If yes, then you may have a worker-scheduling constraint.

Are there times when no work is available?
If yes, then your unit may need flextime or cross-training.

Do some employees have a lot to do and others little?
If yes, then you may have a work-distribution constraint.

Worker Competence Constraints

Are some employees meeting goals while others are not?
If yes, selection or training constraints are possible.

Can some workers perform the work after training and others not?
If yes, then there may be a worker-selection constraint.

Do some recruiters or hiring practices produce more productive or more loyal employees?
If yes, then there may be a worker-selection constraint.

Do most employees require extensive training due to a lack of previous training or experience?
If yes, then there may be a worker-selection constraint.

Have the employees received any training?
If no, then there may be a worker-training constraint.

Did the training produce any measurable increases in performance?
If no, then there may be a worker-training constraint.

Work-Resources Constraints

Do employees ever have to stop working to wait for supplies?
If yes, then there may be a supplies constraint.

Do the supplies meet the job requirements?
If no, then there may be a supplies constraint.

Is the equipment in good working order?
If no, then there may be tools constraints.

Are the right tools and equipment available and in working order?
If no, then there may be tools constraints.

Is there a significant amount of equipment downtime or tool failure?
If no, then there may be tools constraints.

Work-Processes Constraints

Do employees consistently run out of work?
If yes, then job-design (job-enlargement) constraints are a possibility.

Are employees delayed due to decisions that must be made by someone else?
If yes, then job-design (job-enrichment) constraints are a possibility.

Is there a variation in the way that different employees do the same job?
If yes, then job-methods constraints are possible constraints.

Has there been a recent change in job methods, work input, or technology?
If yes, then job-methods constraints are possible.

Prompting Constraints

Are work assignments not accomplished?
If yes, then missing or ambiguous prompts may be constraints.

Could your employees explain to a new employee what their job involves?
If no, then missing or ambiguous prompts may be constraints.

Are job components that follow a series of sequential steps performed out of order?
If yes, then missing or ambiguous prompts may be constraints.

Are there any new procedures or critical procedures that employees tend to "forget"?
If yes, then missing or ambiguous prompts may be constraints.

Do employees have manuals or job aids? Would employees be more efficient or effective if these were available?

If yes, then missing or ambiguous prompts may be constraints.

Feedback Constraints

If you asked good or poor employees how they are performing, would they respond accurately?

If no, feedback may be a constraint.

Are work assignments accomplished but are late or don't meet requirements?

If yes, feedback may be a constraint.

If there is something positive or negative about an employee's work, is an immediate comment from the supervisor likely?

If no, feedback may be a constraint.

Do some employees receive feedback more frequently than others?

If yes, feedback may be a constraint.

When feedback is provided, is it to the work group rather than individuals?

If yes, feedback may be a constraint.

When feedback is provided to employees about their work, are performance improvement suggestions provided?

If no, feedback may be a constraint.

Do employees look forward to feedback from the supervisor and organization?
If no, feedback may be a constraint.

Is the percentage of positive comments made to employees greater than neutral or negative comments?
If no, feedback may be a constraint.

Consequence Constraints

When employees are provided prompts and feedback, is the work still late or of poor quality?
If yes, the consequences of performance may be a constraint.

When an employee performs well, or makes mistakes, are there typically immediate consequences?
If no, the consequences of performance may be a constraint.

Are there competing consequences that prevent getting the job done? Are there positive but also negative consequences for performing well?
If yes, the consequences of performance may be a constraint.

Are there no consequences or positive consequences for engaging in non-work-related activities?
If yes, the consequences of performance may be a constraint.

When an employee performs well, or makes a mistake, does it typically take a long time for the consequences for these actions to occur?
If yes, the consequences of performance may be a constraint.

After around 30 minutes, both Emily and Elaine looked up and signaled they were ready to discuss the items. Emily spoke first. "These are the questions that I feel are problems in my area that affect order input accuracy."

Opportunity Constraints
Is work returned by your unit to a sending or upstream unit?
Is the upstream unit's work arrival often late?

Capability Constraints
Is the equipment in good working order?

Context Constraints
When feedback is provided, is it to the work group rather than individuals?
When feedback is provided to employees about their work, are performance improvement suggestions provided?

Juanita responded, "To remove the opportunity constraints you listed, we'll have to change behaviors in other departments. To reduce the capability constraints, we would need to increase computer-response time and up-time. But to reduce the feedback constraint, you only need to change what you are doing."

"That seems the quickest and easiest. Let's work on that constraint first," Emily said.

Elaine spoke next. "These are the questions I thought were pertinent to my salespeople's prospecting."

Opportunity Constraints
Do some employees have a lot to do and others little?

Capability Constraints
Have the employees received any training?
Do employees ever have to stop working to wait for supplies?

Context Constraints
Are work assignments not accomplished?
When feedback is provided, is it to the work group rather than individuals?
When an employee performs well, or makes mistakes, are there typically immediate consequences?

Juanita continued, "Elaine, two of your constraints have to do with the development and distribution of prospecting leads since you meant by supplies that they didn't have leads to follow. Without sufficient leads, capability and context constraints don't mean much. I'd suggest we improve the prospect-lead generation and distribution procedures. What do you think?"

"I agree, but think we also need to improve the feedback. Is there some way to combine the two?" Elaine asked.

Juanita answered, "Yes, instead of salespeople deciding which leads, and how many leads, to pursue, you could give them a list of leads at the beginning of the month. At the end of each week, you could see how many of the leads they had followed up on as a percentage of the total list they received. The percentage would be your feedback measure."

"Great idea!" Elaine replied.

Juanita then said, "This afternoon, I'll review with you the different types of performance improvement projects and how they relate to the performance constraints you identify in your areas."

Performance Improvement Plans

1. Select improvement target from scorecard
2. Define critical behaviors as needed
3. Pinpoint performance constraints
4. **Design or select performance improvement plan**
5. Conduct cost-benefit analysis

Juanita handed out packets to Emily and Elaine. She then said, "These packets contain brief descriptions of the 16 performance improvement plans described in the constraint-analysis table. Please read them over and ask questions if any don't make sense. Emily you should look at the feedback plans and Elaine the work distribution and resource plans. I'll give you some time to review the plans then we'll talk."

Elaine and Emily began reading through the performance improvement plan descriptions.

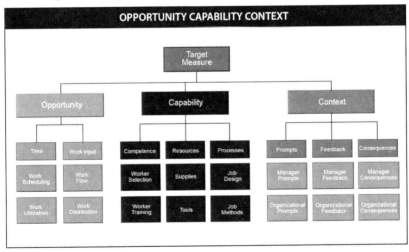

Constraint	Performance Improvement Plan
1. Work Scheduling	**Work Forecasting:** Work forecasts are conducted to predict future volume. **Employee Scheduling:** Schedules are based upon work forecasts. **Flex Time:** Work schedules are matched to work availability. **Job Sharing:** Employees share a job and synchronize work schedules. **Ride Sharing, Wellness:** Transportation and wellness programs are developed.
2. Utilization	**Cross Utilization:** Employees move to other areas when work is unavailable. **Work Prospecting:** Additional work is brought into the department. **Attendance Policies, Incentives:** Positive and negative reinforcement is given for attendance.
3. Workflow	**Cross-functional Teams:** Upstream, downstream, and support departments meet. **Linked Scorecards:** Downstream performances are included in upstream department's scorecard.
4. Work Distribution	**Short-interval Scheduling:** Work to be distributed is organized into equivalent, standard time batches.

5. Worker Selection	**Work Samples:** The employee completes a work-samples selection process. **Structured Interviews:** Interviews include an objective, weighted interviewer form.
6. Worker Training	**Mentoring:** Trainees are assigned a coach. **Simulation:** Trainees participate in job simulation. **Modeling:** Trainees observe and imitate live or video models.
7. Work Supplies	**Inventory Management:** Supply parts and cycle counts are implemented.
8. Work Tools	**Preventive Maintenance:** A maintenance checklist and schedule are implemented.
9. Job Design	**Job Enrichment and Enlargement:** More decision authority is assigned to employees or job duties are expanded.
10. Job Methods	**Methods Improvement:** The work process is simplified.
11. Manager Prompts	**Performance Management Training**
12. Organizational Prompts	**Organizational Communications:** Job descriptions and organizational communications are improved.

13. Manager Feeback	**Performance Management Training**
14. Organizational Feedback	**Performance Scorecards:** Objective, monthly scorecards
15. Manager Consequences	**Performance Management Training**
16. Organizational Consequences	**Performance Recognition and Pay**

Emily spoke up, "I went to the manager training session and understand that I might need to give better feedback. Do you have any ideas?"

Juanita thought a minute and said, "We are already tracking accuracy on the scorecards, but it is monthly feedback, which may be too delayed to improve your employees' accuracy by itself. Maybe you could come up with an error-classification system and count the number of each type of error. Once you find out what the most common errors are, you could provide your employees a training session and a 'cheat sheet' on how to process the input that produces the most errors. Finally, you could review each employee's errors at the end of each week and make sure they individually understand the correct processing procedure."

"Very thorough and very doable," Emily exclaimed. "I can imagine the party we'll have when we receive our $100 checks."

Elaine, the sales manager, cleared her throat and said, "In the distribution-improvement plan it mentions standard time. I don't really know what that is."

Juanita answered, "It is the average time it takes to complete a task. In your case, it is the time it takes to make an appointment and visit a prospect. You will need to put a time estimate on each new lead and then distribute the leads such that each salesperson has about the same total time assigned each month."

Elaine responded with obvious enthusiasm, "I never really considered how long a prospect call took. Prospects have different travel times and more or less complex supply needs. I just handed them out to people haphazardly. Just doing what you say will likely increase the percentage of the prospect list each salesperson completes!"

"Right," Juanita agreed. But you'll also sit down with each salesperson weekly and review what percentage of the list they completed. You can then work with those who are falling behind by performing a constraint analysis on their individual situations. If any do fall behind, it might be due to an inability to make appointments, other tasks that prevent prospecting, or poor travel routing and arrangements."

Elaine turned to Emily and said, "Maybe we can have our award parties together?"

"Sounds great," Emily responded.

Performance Improvement Plans

1. Select improvement target from scorecard
2. Define critical behaviors as needed
3. Pinpoint performance constraints
4. Design or select performance improvement plan
5. Conduct cost-benefit analysis

"Okay," Juanita said. "The last step in a performance improvement project is a cost/benefit analysis. However, neither of your projects involves any significant expenses. A cost/benefit analysis is conducted for projects with substantial expenses like training, equipment, automation, and so on. Therefore, we won't conduct one for either of these projects but may need to for other managers' projects."

Level II: Stakeholder Pay

The 15 managers and supervisors, with Juanita's help, all designed and implemented performance improvement projects over the next three weeks. Four of the target performances achieved a minimum 30 percent improvement within the first month while eight other projects achieved the goal improvement within the 90-day requirement. A number of performance constraints were removed and the total effort had a good effect on the organization's bottom line.

As importantly, the projects set the stage for the transition to Level II: Stakeholder Pay. Managers and workers began to focus on results and were positively reinforced for achieving successful improvements. These successes gave many employees a heightened sense of empowerment over their jobs and tasks. Finally, managers and subordinates worked together as a team and were rewarded as a team.

The transition team, Sid, the CEO; Jim, the consultant from the bank; Margaret, CFO; Julie, the HR Director; Larry, the plant manager; Elaine, the sales manager; and Juanita, the quality assurance manager; met to discuss the strategy for moving the organization to Level II: Stakeholder Pay.

Jim began, "The transition plan is to introduce Profit-Indexed Performance Pay (PIPP) next month. The PIPP formula for computing monthly payouts is as follows:

Base Pay	X	Opportunity %	X	Profit Multiplier	X	Performance Index	=	Payout
$2,000	X	4%	X	1.0	X	60%	=	$48

"The base pay is the monthly salary or the month's hourly earnings including overtime pay," Jim explained.

Step 1: Assigning Performance Pay Opportunity Percent

Base Pay	X	Opportunity %	X	Profit Multiplier	X	Performance Index	=	Payout
$2,000	X	4%	X	1.0	X	60%	=	$48

"Every employee will be assigned a percentage of their base pay they can earn in performance pay. The opportunity percentage is initially based on the anticipated annual base-pay increase since it will replace it. What is your plan for the coming year?"

Julie responded, "We were planning to give an average 4 percent annual increase this coming year."

"Okay," Jim said. "Then make the minimum guaranteed opportunity 4 percent and the maximum three times that or 12 percent. By substituting performance pay for an increase in guaranteed base pay, employees will immediately have a stake in the game."

"That doesn't seem like much money," Elaine complained. "If my salespeople's commissions are going to be replaced by PIPP they'll all look for other work!"

Jim replied, "For employees who previously participated in performance pay or bonus programs we will adjust their opportunity percentage to reflect those earnings. What percent of their base pay do your salespeople earn annually?"

Elaine replied, "Around 20 percent."

"Then their opportunity percentage would be 20 percent plus 4 percent or 24 percent with a maximum of 72 percent," Jim stated.

"Wow, that's a lot more then they earn now!" exclaimed Elaine.

"Yeah, but remember we are asking a lot more from them," Jim counseled. "On the commission they were only accountable for monthly revenue. On the scorecard, in addition to monthly revenue, they have to control the gross margin percentage, DIO, and account attrition. We're asking a lot more and offering a lot more. Also remember that the payout opportunity is indexed to the company's profit.

"Since there are no other bonus programs, all other employees will be assigned a 4 percent opportunity," Jim continued. Also, if any job group is below market, you might want to consider raising their opportunity percentage to adjust for this. Now let's talk about the second element in computing performance pay opportunity—the profit multiplier."

Base Pay	X	Opportunity %	X	Profit Multiplier	X	Performance Index	=	Payout
$2,000	X	4%	X	1. 0	X	60%	=	$48

The Profit Multiplier

Jim began, "There are three components to the profit multiplier: the threshold, the share percentage, and the cap. The threshold is computed as the cost of guaranteed (not profit-indexed) performance pay opportunity. For example, let's say we offer a 4 percent minimum guaranteed performance pay opportunity and the monthly payroll averages $150,000. Then the monthly threshold would be $150,000 X 4%= $6,000. You might also consider owner pay, debt pay down, and building a cash reserve in defining your threshold. Sid and Margaret, what do you think the profit-multiplier threshold should be?"

Margaret began, "Well, we have a sizeable debt so that should be included. Sid takes a salary above the profit line, like everyone else, and plows all the profits into the company so we don't need to cover that. I'd say if we could put away $4,000 a month plus cover the $6,000 in guaranteed performance pay opportunity we'd be good."

Sid chimed in, "Makes sense to me."

Jim wrapped up by saying, "Good. The profit-multiplier threshold will be $10,000 a month. Margaret, how many months last year did we make at least a $10,000 profit?"

"I have our P&L here; let me look," Margaret responded. "We only made $10,000 or more in six of the twelve months."

Jim said, "That's sufficient. There would only be a problem if it was three or fewer months. In that case, we'd have to lower the threshold for the plan to have an impact.

"The next step in computing the profit multiplier is the share percentage. The share percentage is the percentage of every profit dollar above threshold that is used to fund the performance pay plan," Jim explained. "One method for computing the share percentage is to divide the total annual payroll by the total annual revenue. This tells you how much of each revenue dollar you have shared in the past. What is this percentage, Margaret?"

Margaret took out her calculator and computed the percentage. "We have an annual payroll of $1.8 million and an annual revenue of $4.8 million. That comes out to 37.5 percent."

Jim thought and said, "Let's round it to 40 percent. 40 percent will be our share percentage.

"Now, the last step is to compute the profit we need for a profit multiplier of one. We compute the performance opportunity cost as base salaries multiplied by opportunity percentages. Everyone has a 4 percent opportunity except the salespeople who have a 24 percent opportunity, since we are replacing their commission plan.

$1,500,000 X 4% = $60,000
$300,000 X 24%= $72,000
$132,000 / 40% = $330,000 / 12 months = $27,500.

"The monthly opportunity cost is $132,000. We then divide this by the share percentage to compute the profit required for a performance pay profit multiplier of 1. 00. We then convert the annual multiplier to a monthly multiplier by dividing by 12. Finally, we add the threshold of $10,000 to the multiplier to compute the final multiplier at 1. 0."

Jim continued, "Let's round that to $30,000. Our profit-multiplier calculation each month will be as follows:

Threshold	Profit Multiplier of 1
$10,000	$30,000 + $10,000 = $40,000

"To compute each month's profit multiplier we take the rolling three-month average profit and apply it in this formula. In this example, let's say our profit is $50,000." Jim went to the whiteboard and wrote

(3MMA Profit -Threshold) /1 Profit Multiplier - Threshold)
= Profit Multiplier

($50,000 - $10,000) / ($40,000 - $10,000)
= $40,000 / $30,000 = 1. 33

Jim continued, "For employees with a 4 percent basis, their performance pay opportunity percentage will be 4 percent X 1. 33 = 5. 32 percent. For the salespeople it will be 24 percent X 1. 33 = 31. 92 percent. These percentages will be multiplied by the employee's monthly base pay to compute the dollar amount of performance pay opportunity."

Larry, the plant manager, finally spoke up. "What if the profit were $200,000?" he asked.

Jim wrote:

($200,000 - $10,000) / ($40,000 - $10,000)
= $190,000 / $30,000 = 6. 33

Jim went on, "Larry's calculation brings up our last issue in developing Superior Button's PIPP. That is, should the performance pay opportunity be capped? We recommend capping the profit multiplier at 3. 00. By doing so, you can raise the cap when you increase the scorecard goals or when you further leverage employee base pay. At the bank, we've finished these processes and have removed the cap."

Sid said, "Sounds like a good idea. That way we won't set any false employee expectations and can control the transition."

"Exactly," Jim agreed.

Jim summarized, "Superior Button will begin its Profit-Indexed Performance Pay System with a performance pay opportunity of 4 percent for all employees except salespeople who will be assigned a 24 percent opportunity to replace their commission plan. There will be a profit-multiplier scale that ranges from $10,000 = 0 to $40,000 = 1. 00. There will be a 3. 00 cap on the scale in the beginning. That is, no additional payments will be made beyond a $100,000 monthly profit ($10,000 + 30,000 + 30,000, + 30,000). The profit will be computed as a three-month rolling average. Payouts will be monthly and paid the second week of the following month. A complete monthly payout formula example is as follows:

Base Pay	X	Opportunity %	X	Profit Multiplier	X	Performance Index	=	Payout
$3,000	X	4%	X	2. 0	X	60%	=	$144

"Any questions?"

Sid asked, "What is the next transition step?"

"We'll talk about next steps tomorrow, if that's okay with you," Jim replied.

"Fine," Sid sighed, "I've had enough for one day."

Chapter 21

Level II: Implementing Stakeholder Pay

Yesterday's project group returned to the meeting room, got their coffee and doughnuts, and took their seats. Jim stood up and began, "I know yesterday was challenging due to all of the math involved. You'll be pleased to know that today's topic, stakeholder pay, is more conceptual and less about numbers."

An audible sigh of relief could be heard around the table. Jim continued, "Stakeholder pay expands Profit-Indexed Performance Pay in that it is concerned with employees taking a risk by lowering their base pay in exchange for an opportunity to share in more of the company's success. In a real sense, they become investors in Superior Button. Stakeholder pay is based on Profit-Indexed Performance Pay. The stakeholder decision for an employee is to increase their opportunity percentage by lowering their base pay."

Larry spoke up, "Why would anyone want to do that?"

Jim replied, "Because for every dollar of base pay an employee gives up, three dollars are added to the PIPP opportunity percentage. Put another way, the employee receives a three-to-one return on every dollar of base pay they invest."

Sid entered the discussion, "That's a 300 percent return on investment. Seems like everyone would want to do that. They could triple their pay! How could we possibly afford it?"

226 · Level II: Implementing Stakeholder Pay

"Remember," Jim said, "under PIPP the only way all employee pay would triple is if Superior Button's profits tripled and the employees consistently scored 100 percent on their scorecards."

Julie joined the discussion. "So the employee has to have faith that our profits will improve, and that they will be able to perform consistently well on their scorecard, before they would be willing to take the risk?"

Jim responded, "Correct, but there is another issue. They also have to have faith that the new pay system will be reliable. That is, management won't arbitrarily change the scorecard goals or the profit-share formula. I will pass out a summary of the issues employees consider in moving from conventional, guaranteed base pay to stakeholder pay." Jim passed out the following sheet.

Personal Risk Factors

• Skills (Can I do it?)

• Investment (Do I have too much at stake?)

Organizational Risk Factors

• Effort (Are the goals attainable?)

• Faith (Will the company succeed?)

• Trust (Will I really share in the success?)

• Opportunity (Will I have the chance to share?)

• Help (Will others cooperate?)

"The employees have been receiving their scorecards for four months now and have a good idea if they have the skills to meet their goals. You can help those employees who are not meeting their goals to improve their skills through training and mentoring, and through implementing performance improvement projects," Jim instructed. "The second personal risk issue, investment, is more difficult to address. Most managers assume that professionals and managers would be the first to volunteer for a stakeholder position. This turns out not to be the case in many instances. In fact, it has proven generally more likely that the lowest-paid employees will be the first to volunteer to become stakeholders."

"Why is that, again?" Larry asked.

Jim replied, "Because they have the least to lose and the most to gain in a stakeholder plan. They are only risking a minimum wage where managers and professionals have invested in their higher pay through education and career advancement over a period of time. Many minimum-wage employees are well aware that their backgrounds prevent them from rising through the conventional ranks into management. Their pay is pretty much fixed in place."

"Okay, then why would a manager want to make the shift?" Larry asked.

"Managers generally understand the factors involved in an organization's profitability and are in a better position to impact it," Jim responded. "Also, tripling a high salary is considerably more money than tripling a low one."

Jim continued, "The organizational risk factors are much more under management control. You can resolve the effort issue by setting achievable goals and, more importantly, by not arbitrarily making them more difficult as performance improves. You can affect the employees' faith in the company's future success by instituting Open Book Management and sharing financial information and strategies with all employees. You can instill trust in the system by developing and sharing policies for when the system will be changed and sticking to them.

"We have already made progress in the opportunity risks factor in our Level I implementation. Managers and workers have removed a number of performance constraints in their performance improvement projects. They have also worked as teams, which improves the help factor."

Jim continued, "There are two proven strategies for a transition from conventional pay to stakeholder pay. The first is a base pay freeze and the second is a voluntary, base-pay reduction program. You could also institute some combination of these two approaches. Let me first explain the base-pay freeze approach to moving toward stake-holder pay. The basic idea is to discontinue annual base-pay increases and instead increase performance pay opportunity. This strategy looks like this."

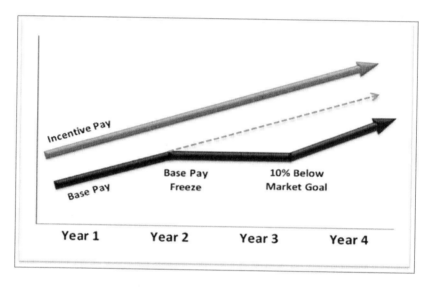

Jim instructed, "The dotted line represents what your competitors are paying. As you can see, the base pay falls below market while the performance pay, since it is added at a 3:1 ratio, puts your good performing employees well above market. The sample organization has elected to end the base-pay freeze when employees are 10 percent below market."

Julie, concerned, said, "We won't be able to hire anyone if we are too far below market!"

"That's not what our experience shows," Jim replied. "What will happen is that you will attract a different kind of employee. You are telling the job applicant that if they perform poorly they will make below market; if they are average performers they will make market; and if they are good performers they will make well above market. If they don't want the job under these conditions, have you really lost much?"

"I see," Julie said. "Stakeholder pay is, in a sense, a selection strategy."

"Right," Jim replied admiringly.

"Let me pass out this sheet so we can look at the actual impact of a base-pay freeze concurrent with an annual increase in performance pay opportunity.

Year	Typical Pay Increase (4%)	Base-Pay Freeze	% Market	Incentive Opportunity	Low Performer	High Performer
1	$30,000	$30,000	100%	8%	$30,720	$32,400
2	$31,200	$30,000	96%	16%	$31,440	$34,800
3	$32,448	$30,000	92%	24%	$32,160	$37,200
4	$33,745	$30,000	88%	32%	$32,880	$39,600
5	$35,095	$30,000	81%	40%	$33,600	$42,000

"You can see that by year five the organization has reduced its pay guarantee for an employee with a $30,000 salary by over $5,000. In the fifth year the employees are at about 80 percent of market. However, the incentive opportunity has increased to 40 percent of base pay. Low performers are earning $33,600 instead of the $35,095 they would have earned in the conventional pay system. High performers are earning $42,000 as opposed to the $35,095 they would have earned in the conventional system. Employees who average 50 percent on the scorecard will earn at market.

"Stakeholder pay redistributes the payroll such that high performers make more and poor performers less. Is this fair?" Julie asked.

Sid chimed in, "Of course it is! The conventional pay system pays everyone about the same regardless of their performance—that isn't fair and it isn't motivating."

"I agree," Jim said. "The conventional system treats employees like commodities. That is, one loaf of bread is like another so the price is set entirely by the market. Stakeholder pay recognizes and rewards individual initiative and pays for what you do rather than who you are.

"There is a second strategy for a transition to stakeholder pay that has also proven successful. It is a voluntary, pay-leveraging program. Employees volunteer to give up all, or a significant portion, of base pay, in exchange for a three-to-one increase in their personal performance pay opportunity percentage." Jim went to the whiteboard and wrote the following list:

Pay-Leveraging Strategy

1. Phase-in when profit-indexed performance pay is reliable.
2. Only top-scorecard performers are eligible to volunteer.
3. Each 1 percent of salary given up is offset by a 3 percent increase in performance pay opportunity.
4. Provide a three- to six-month grace period in which employees can opt out of leverage pay.
5. Managers ensure employees have the opportunity to perform.
6. The organization's strategy and future performance must be marketed to the new stakeholders.

"This voluntary leveraging program can be implemented instead of the base-pay freeze or in addition to the freeze," Jim stated. "Only top-scorecard performers are eligible to volunteer. This ensures that volunteers will be winners and encourages others to volunteer. The conditions of volunteering are that, during a grace period, the employee can choose to return to the conventional system. Once the grace period is over, they will be unable to switch back. In our experience, none of the stakeholders chose to return to conventional pay and an increasing number of other employees wished to volunteer."

"That surprises me," Elaine commented.

"It did us too," Jim responded. "But that's because we were only thinking about money. Moving to stakeholder pay is not just a financial decision. It is a chance to take control of your work life and to regain the natural connection between effort and results. People take risks all the time when they move to self-employment. Why? We don't think it is all about money. It is about returning to our natural state where what we do directly influences what happens to us."

Larry entered the discussion. "So a transition to stakeholder pay isn't just about money or time off; it's about employee empowerment and self-worth!" he said.

"Exactly!" Jim said excitedly. "Stakeholder pay is a psychological transformation, not just a change in pay, which brings up a point I should make. Stakeholder pay *will* change your employees' approach to work. Let me give you an example with our tellers at the bank. Before the transition, tellers were all paid about the same. If they showed up for work they earned their hourly wage. However, if their cash drawers didn't balance at the end of the day, they were reprimanded and, if that result was repeated, they were terminated. It was a classic case of 'show up and don't screw up' management. Under this management system, what do you think tellers thought of customers?"

Elaine responded, "I guess they saw customers as nothing more than a chance to screw up. Especially those they thought would have complicated transactions."

"Yeah," Jim replied, "And those were usually our best customers! Basically, if you completed a minimum number of transactions accurately, you were safe from adverse outcomes. We had numerous customer service training sessions and a customer service survey but none of it overcame this fundamental flaw in our pay system. When we installed stakeholder pay, the teller behaviors changed in only a few days. They now saw customers as opportunities since they were paid for the number of transactions they processed. We eventually took the queue ropes down and let customers choose who served them. You could walk into the bank lobby and tell who the friendliest and most efficient tellers were from the length of their queues.

"Another interesting development, that we didn't anticipate, was the effect of stakeholder pay on teller staffing and scheduling. With conventional pay, tellers were always asking for additional tellers and wanted to work on days when customer traffic was low. With stakeholder pay, all this reversed quickly. The tellers quit requesting new tellers even when a teller left the bank. Further, they requested the high customer traffic days. In both cases, they were simply trying to maximize their transactions and performance pay."

Jim continued, "Some managers are concerned that the introduction of stakeholder pay will cause a number of employees to leave the organization. That's not what we found—just the opposite."

"We tracked employee attrition for the first seven years of the program and found that it dropped substantially. We also found that under-time, showing up late or leaving early, was significantly reduced. Both these effects make sense. People prefer to work where they are empowered and there is no limit on their potential earnings. People tend to show up and stay the full day to maximize their earnings for the day. In fact, we had employees coming in early and we had to implement a policy that no one could start work until 8:00 a. m.! The following comparison summarizes the differences between conventional entitlement pay and stakeholder pay."

Entitlement	Stakeholder
• Pay for time	• Pay for results
• Direct Supervision	• Facilitation
• Pay range set by market	• Pay range set by performance and profit
• Performance-based promotions	• No cap on earnings in each job
• Company does not share profit	• Company shares profit gains and does not lay off when profit declines
• Gains and lays off in bad times	

Jim continued, "We have talked about the problems with pay for time and traditional, direct-supervision bureaucracies. We've also talked about the poor practice of promoting good performers as a reward for their good performance. But we have not discussed another major benefit of stakeholder pay to both the organization and its employees. This benefit is moving from a fixed-cost payroll to a variable-cost payroll. Traditional wages and salaries are basically a fixed cost to an organization. They remain about the same in good times and bad times. Stakeholder pay is indexed to the organization's profitability. In good times the payroll increases while in bad times it decreases.

In conventional pay, when revenues are up, there is more work to do, but the payroll remains the same. When revenues are down, employees are laid off to preserve profitability. The employee loses in good times and bad times. Furthermore, the practice of annual base-pay increases will reduce profitability unless the company can consistently raise prices to offset the increases. Stakeholder pay is an alternative to the conventional compensation system and indexes pay to profit. This stabilizes the organization's profit margin but also benefits employees in good times and bad times." Jim wrote the following list on the whiteboard and resumed, "This list summarizes the benefits of a transition from conventional pay to stakeholder pay," he stated.

1. **More equitably distributes pay to high performers**
2. **Better aligns employees' personal financial interests with the organization's**
3. **Protects employee jobs during business downturns**
4. **Ensures pay affordability**
5. **Ensures performance measurement system integrity by indexing performance pay to organizational profitability; (self-regulating)**

Chapter 22

Level III: Job Enrichment Program

A year after implementation, the project team; Sid, Margaret, Julie, Larry, Elaine, and Juanita met with Jim to discuss the transition to Level III: Job Enrichment. The Stakeholder Pay System had been in place for six months. Of the 67 employees working at Superior Button, all had their annual 4 percent pay increase added to their performance pay opportunity percentage rather than their base pay. All of Larry's 23 plant employees volunteered to have their base pay replaced with performance pay. They were in the third month of this arrangement with the understanding they could choose to return to the original pay system at the end of the sixth month.

Jim inquired, "Larry, how is the performance pay working out in the plant?"

Larry responded, "Most of them really like it, and all but one of them are earning higher pay than before."

"Any problems?" Jim asked.

Larry said, "One major problem, we didn't used to have, is that when they run out of work they are upset because it lowers their earnings for the day. They also are complaining that the raw materials we're purchasing for the buttons are too brittle and create a lot of scrap and returns. These are complaints I've never had before, but I see how the performance pay would create these new concerns. They constrain performance on measures 1, 2, 4, and 5 on their scorecards."

Production Cutter (reports to Cutting Supervisor) (8)

Measure	Min	Max	Priority Weight
(1) Scrap Expense / Revenue	17%	5%	10%
(2) Lbs / Production Labor Hr.	1.65	2.40	25%
(3) Behavior Safety Checklist%	80%	100%	25%
(4) % Orders on Time	74%	100%	20%
(5) % Returns	7%	3%	20%

Production Finisher (reports to Finishing Supervisor) (7)

Measure	Min	Max	Priority Weight
(1) Scrap Expense / Revenue	17%	5%	15%
(2) Lbs / Production Labor Hr.	.60	.90	30%
(3) Behavior Safety Checklist%	80%	100%	15%
(4) % Orders on Time	74%	100%	20%
(5) % Returns	7%	3%	20%

Jim replied, "These issues are exactly why we are moving to Level III: Job Enrichment. There are three chief strategies used in job enrichment as we define it. They are job redesign, flexible scheduling, and cross utilization.

"Job redesign involves both job enlargement and job empowerment.

"Job enlargement is expanding the number of job tasks within a job position, while job empowerment transfers decision-making authorities to the worker. For example, Larry, is there any reason that cutters could not be trained as finishers and vice versa? If the jobs were consolidated, the employees could move to where the work is rather than the finishers waiting for the cutters to complete their job."

Jim continued, "A further advantage to this approach is that absences or unexpected volume surges will have less impact on the area meeting its deadlines."

Larry began to see the advantages and said, "Sounds good. But what if they don't want to learn the new job?"

Jim responded, "That was a problem when job enlargement was attempted in organizations that had a conventional wage-and-salary system. However, in your stakeholder system, job enlargement equates to more performance pay opportunity so employee receptivity is generally good.

"You also have a cutter and a finishing supervisor. If we combine the jobs, there will be 15 production employees. Could one supervisor manage these employees?"

"Yes," Larry replied hesitantly, "But they will have to work harder to supervise both functions with twice as many employees. Also, what happens to the supervisor that is not put in charge of both functions?"

"We could raise the new supervisor's performance pay opportunity percentage to reward taking on a larger span of control," Jim pointed out. "We could wait till a supervisor in another area leaves the company and place one of the supervisors there. Or, one of the supervisors might want to return to production with the new performance pay system. Were either of your supervisors promoted from worker to supervisor?"

Larry said, "Both of them moved up from production."

Jim asked, "Were both of them promoted because they were good workers?"

"Yes," Larry replied. "And because they were top performers they would likely make the same money as a worker that they now make as a supervisor. Denny, the finishing supervisor, has never liked supervision and isn't very good at it. He might jump at the chance to return to production at which he is very good."

Jim said, "Sounds like a plan." He continued, "Let's talk about job empowerment. You said that the scrap and return rates were high because of poor quality raw materials."

"That's right," Larry replied. "My people are constantly complaining about this, but they have to work with what they are given."

Jim inquired, "What if Manos, the purchasing manager, met with members of the production team and provided samples of raw materials he plans to order? The team would have a say in which materials were ordered. This is an example of job empowerment."

Larry replied, "They would have to be conscious of the cost of raw materials, not just the quality."

"Two factors make this concern likely," Jim said. "First, we are measuring scrap expense in dollars compared to revenue. Less expensive raw material scrap will improve their scrap ratio. Second, the performance pay opportunity is indexed to profit. Lower cost raw materials will improve profitability assuming the quality is satisfactory. Of course, you would have to make the production team aware of these contingencies. Also, is it ever the case that Manos has to special order raw materials because production runs and deadlines weren't shared with him?"

"He says it happens all the time," Larry said excitedly. "If the production team had input to purchasing they would also keep Manos more up to date on upcoming runs and deadlines. That would improve his performance by not having to pay more for special orders. It seems to be a win-win situation for both parties!"

"Great!" Jim declared. "We've talked about job enlargement as a method of job enrichment; now let's talk about flexible scheduling. As we talked about in our earlier meetings, there are two benefits to a stakeholder system. Employees can earn more but they also can earn the same and spend less time at work. High performance can be reinforced with more pay or with less time at work. If we combine the two jobs and work cooperatively with purchasing, is it likely that the 15 production employees will have times when there is not enough work for all of them?"

Larry observed, "Well, the finishers will no longer have to wait on the cutters to complete their tasks, so that will free up some time. Even now, however, there are periods of time when neither group has much work to do."

"What if they could delay coming to work or go home early during these periods?" Jim asked.

"They wouldn't want to do that because it would reduce their hours and pay," Larry complained.

"You are forgetting that they volunteered for 100 percent performance pay. They are paid for what they produce, not how many hours they spend producing it. They are paid for results, not time," Jim explained.

Larry said hesitantly, "So, it doesn't matter how many hours they work, only how much they produce. Therefore, when there is nothing to do, they would just as soon be at home!"

"Exactly," Jim confirmed. They can earn at least the same pay as they did on the wage plan but work fewer hours. For many employees, the free time is as much a benefit as the increased pay."

We'd have to develop a good work forecast and work-scheduling system for this to happen," Larry said.

"Right, but the benefits far outweigh this effort. Don't you agree?" Jim asked.

"It all makes sense to me, but it's really different than what we used to do," Larry replied.

Chapter 23

Level III: Cross-Utilization and Lateral-Career Paths

All the senior managers attended the cross-utilization session. This was so because cross-utilization can occur across departments as well as within them.

Jim began, "The last strategy for job enrichment is cross-utilization where people learn tasks in other jobs and move to those jobs during downtime in their own job. This strategy has been tried by many organizations and has been termed *skills-based pay*. Unfortunately, the results were mixed because salaries were increased for learning a skill rather than applying the skill. Since there was no incentive to apply the skill, in many cases the outcome was only an increase in payroll cost. We will be rewarding actual cross-utilization rather than simply learning new skills."

"How does it work?" Larry asked.

Jim told Larry, "Cross-utilization is when an employee has little work to do in his area, so he moves to another area where there is ample work to do. Of course, to be cross-utilized you also have to be cross-trained."

He said, "Cross-training should occur between areas that have opposite work-input cycles or from a cyclic area to one that has a constant volume. Areas for cross-utilization should be selected that have job functions that require a minimum of experience or training and are not critical priorities for the areas."

Jim continued, "There are four types of measures that encourage and reward employees for cross-utilization." The four types that he explained are as follows:

1. *Loaned hour's scorecard measure*—The simplest approach is to add up the hours an employee has worked in other units and add it as a scorecard measure. The drawbacks to this approach are it is difficult to verify and there is no guarantee that useful work will be performed in the other areas.

2. *Dual scorecards*— For employees who are assigned to job A, but work a significant portion of their time in Job B, you can create two scorecards for the employee—one for job A and one for job B. Each month you multiply each scorecard by the hours worked in the job and divide by the total work hours to compute a weighted performance index. For example:
(80% X 120 hours) + (40% X 40 hours) = 96 + 16 = 112 / 160 = 70% weighed performance index

3. *Performance credit system*—If you have a standard time system, you can simply add the earned hours from the different job positions.

4. *Team productivity scorecard measure.*

Team work volume =
Team actual hours - loaned + borrowed

Jim continued, "We have had a lot of success with the team score-card approach. The team makes a decision for one or more of its members to work in other job positions. The hours they work outside the team are subtracted from the team's actual hours, which increases the team's productivity ratio. The borrowing teams add the actual hours of the borrowed employees to their team scorecards. The result is the loaned and borrowed hours net to zero. This prevents any inflated loaned hours since the borrowing team will want to use other team's members only when it is to their advantage. The team score-card also sets the stage for Level IV: Self-Managed Employees."

Larry said, "I really like the team idea. It's simple to track and gets the team to work together. How do you set up such a program?"

Jim responded, "There are seven steps to creating a team work-place environment." The seven steps explained by Jim are as follows:

1. *Team Productivity Measure*—Add a team productivity measure to all the scorecards where cross-utilization will be a strategy. Possibly keep individual productivity measures on the scorecard as well, but they may conflict with the team's objectives.

2. *Work Volume Study*—Examine work input and deadlines in all the areas that will cross-utilize employees and look for input cycles that increase and decrease in opposite directions. Also examine deadlines and see when they are most often missed. These periods are good cross-utilization opportunities.

3. *Skills Analysis*—Pinpoint work volumes that require minimal new skills. Also select skills where the cross-utilized employees' pay is the same or lower than the employees in the job for which they will be cross-utilized.

4. *Training Schedule*—Develop training for the identified skills and set up a training schedule for employees who plan to be cross-utilized.

5. *Cross-utilization Opportunity Posting*—Develop a posting system. Either post cross-utilization opportunities on a wall poster that employees can initial, or develop a posting system that displays on the supervisor's computer screen.

6. *Reduce Team Hours*—When employees leave the company, determine if the job they left can be done without a replacement using cross-utilized employees.

7. *Create a Lateral Career Path*—Cross-training is an exciting, alternative-career path to the traditional one of moving up into management. This allows employees to become proficient at more job tasks to increase their pay opportunity rather than having to move into management.

Employees who are certified in multiple skills, and maintain a minimum 20 percent loaned hours, have their performance pay opportunity increased. For example,

Grade I	1 additional skill	1% increase in performance pay opportunity
Grade II	3 additional skills	2% increase in performance pay opportunity
Grade III	7 additional skills	4% increase in performance pay opportunity
Grade IV	10 additional skills	6% increase in performance pay opportunity

Chapter 24

Level IV: Expanding Manager Span of Control

Once Level III was operating successfully, Jim met with the senior management group to discuss the transition to the final level for Superior Button: Self-Managed Teams. "There are many advantages to Superior Button considering the final transition to Level IV: Self-Managed Teams," Jim began. These advantages include the following:

Cost savings—The Company will have less management expense, more productivity, and less turnover.

Innovation—You will have 60 people working on profit improvement rather than just the five senior managers.

Responsiveness—Reducing the company's hierarchical decision process will enable rapid decisions made close to the issue.

Customer Service—Team members focus on customers rather than managers.

Cooperation—Team members will cooperate more.

Jim continued, "Self-managed teams are different from self-directed teams. Your self-managed teams are directed by a common performance scorecard. They don't decide for themselves what is important to the organization."

Julie spoke up, "But what happens to the managers and supervisors we have now?"

"That's what this meeting is about," Jim replied. You are going to implement a plan that rewards increases in the manager span of control across the organization. Management span of control is typically expressed as a ratio of the number of workers divided by the number of managers. At Superior Button you presently have 53 workers and 14 managers and supervisors. Your span of control ratio is 53 /14 = 3.78 or rounded, 4 workers for every manager. The plan is to increase the ratio to at least 10 workers per manager. This will reduce management expenses and set the stage for the self-managed teams."

"How will we do that without causing chaos?" Larry asked suspiciously. "What if a manager increases her span of control but can't really manage all the new employees and functions?"

"Remember," Jim responded, "The manager's performance index is partly based on the performance of their employees. If they exceed their ability to manage, their average employee performance index will decline, which will offset the increase in their larger opportunity percentage."

"Okay," Larry said, somewhat more relaxed, "but what happens to the managers we lose as the span of control increases?"

Jim replied, "We will increase span of control by not rehiring when managers and supervisors leave the company. We'll also allow them to move into the workforce if they wish. Finally, Sid has some ambitious developmental projects to which displaced managers could be reassigned."

"How will we determine which areas a manager will take on?" Julie asked.

"We'll try to organize increases in span of control around common functions, the workflow through the organization, and the training and experience of the managers and supervisors," Jim stated.

Larry said, "I understand common functions like clerical vs. production, but what do you mean by organizing around the workflow?"

Jim responded, "Superior Button has a common workflow throughout the organization. Marketing and sales employees provide purchasing and inventory management with information regarding potential sales. Purchasing orders the raw materials and the warehouse unloads and stocks them. Production uses the materials to make the products which are then moved to the warehouse, loaded on the trucks, and transported." Jim drew the following flowchart.

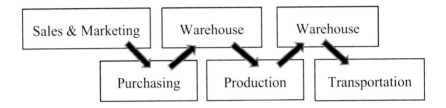

Arthur, the warehouse manager, spoke up for the first time. "What kind of projects does Sid have in mind?"

Sid began to see his new role as planner clearly. He spoke up and said, "I have a number of projects in mind but I've just not had the time to get into them. We have always purchased our raw materials in the United States and our customers, except for one, are all in the U. S. I'd like to expand our sales and purchasing to Europe and Asia. We'd need people to travel around Europe and Asia and find the least expensive, but high quality, materials available. We also would need someone to visit clothing manufacturers in these areas to find new customers. We might also need warehouse facilities in these areas and would need to expand our warehouse here if we secured a lot of new customers.

"I also would like to investigate expanding our product line from just buttons for dress shirts and blouses to jackets, coats, and so on. Someone would need to look into what the market is, who the competitors are, and what equipment and training we'd need to expand our product offerings.

"Another project I have had in mind is developing a website through which prospects could view our products and place orders world-wide."

Sid had mentioned these projects several times over the past two years with only a lukewarm reception from his managers. To his astonishment, his management group actually applauded after he presented his ideas. He was pleased, but temporarily confused, until he realized that these projects would increase profitability which his managers would now share. Before, his ideas meant only more work for the same pay. *I love this liberated organization idea*, he thought. Over the next three months, one manager retired and another added his subordinates to her span of control. A manager and a supervisor volunteered for the product-expansion projects. The span of control moved from $53 / 14 = 3.8$ to $53 / 11 = 4.8$.

Chapter 25

Level IV: Moving to Self-Managed Employees

Self-managed teams are responsible for their scorecard outcomes and benefit from improving these outcomes through stakeholder pay. The teams share and rotate work tasks and managerial duties. They determine how the work is done and distributed among the team members. They also determine team member work schedules. They meet to identify problems and opportunities and develop plans to overcome the problems and realize the opportunities. Some job positions don't require a team and in these cases they become self-managed individuals.

Jim met with Julie, the new performance system manager and HR director, to discuss the transition to Level IV: Self-Managed Employees. He began, "To move toward self-managed teams, some HR policies will need to change. Currently managers and supervisors sign off on vacations, attendance, probations, terminations, work schedules, and purchase orders. We will need to shift these authorities to the teams."

"It's scary, but I see the need," Julie replied.

"The new managers, with their greater spans of control, can make or break the transition," Jim said. "They will be responsible for several self-managed teams. If they continue to manage through traditional command and control, the transition will fail. Fortunately, as a manager's span of control increases, traditional management techniques are less workable. That's why we increase span of control before moving to self-managed teams."

Julie asked, "What will the new managers do differently than before?"

"First, they will serve as a bridge between the senior-management group and the team. They will communicate team ideas and concerns to the management group and in turn will communicate management objectives and concerns to the team," Jim said. "Second, they will coordinate workflow across teams and identify problems and solutions. Third, they will regularly meet with the teams to discuss organizational objectives, successes and failures, and future plans. Finally, they will coach and assist the team leaders in managerial functions. They will gradually transition from the conventional manager role to a facilitator role." Jim went to the whiteboard and wrote the following:

Conventional Management	Self-Managed Teams
• Management authority assigned to manager	• Management authority assigned to team
• Manage employees	• Support and facilitate the team
• Direct and evaluate employee performance	• Scorecards serve this function
• Motivate employees	• Stakeholder Pay

Jim continued, "Teams will either elect a team leader or make decisions consensually. Which method is best will be determined by the team members and the work time frame. If decisions must be made quickly, the team leader approach may be required. Juanita's job, as facilitator, will be to assist the teams in determining which structure they will adopt and to assist those teams who choose to select a team leader. Typically, the first team leader is the most skilled and experienced worker—the person other team members come to with their problems. Juanita will also train the leaders in their new managerial tasks."

"Something has been really bothering me about this transition," Julie said, worried. "In any group of people, some contribute more to the team effort than others. In fact, sometimes a person may contribute little or nothing!"

"Good point," Jim exclaimed. "The free ride or social loafer is often a problem in collective efforts. We plan to address this issue in several ways. First, a team is required only where there is a consistent need for cooperation among a group of people. Many jobs at Superior Button do not require a team. These individuals will be self-managed employees who will be solely responsible for their scorecard performance. Second, where possible, each team scorecard should include at least one measure of individual performance to ensure performance pay is distributed equitably. The measure may be nothing more than attendance or safety. It could also be personal production or errors.

"In some cases, however, a team member may be an adequate performer but other behaviors constrain team performance. These include bullying, arguing, complaining, an unwillingness to mentor other employees, and frequent and extended absences from work. In these instances, the team would have the authority to place an employee on unpaid leave or terminate their employment. You would need to get involved in these decisions to ensure they met employment-law guidelines.

"Some organizations institute a monthly, subjective team evaluation in which team members rate each other's contribution to the team effort. This can either improve the team's effectiveness or seriously undermine it. I suggest this strategy not occur in the initial transition. We'll add it later if it turns out we need it."

"Good idea," Julie agreed.

"Let's compare the old hierarchical organizational structure to the new open system structure," Jim said.

Hierarchical Organizational Structure

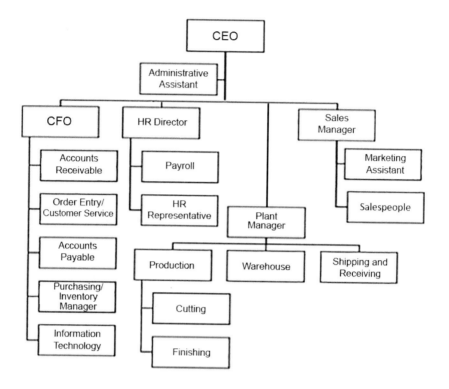

New Network Organizational Structure

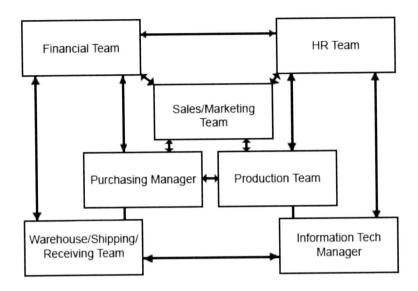

Jim said, "In the broader scope of things, we are creating a self-regulating system where the planner, Sid, studies the marketplace to develop strategies to improve Superior Button's success. These new strategies are communicated to employees through changes in score-card measures and priority weightings made by the PSM. The stakeholders are guided by their scorecard measures. If the strategies are successful, organizational profitability improves, which is shared by all based on their personal or team contribution."

Chapter 26

Results and the Future

Today, it has been just over two years since I first met with Jim and he began helping us implement a liberated workplace at Superior Button. Recently, Jim met with Ellen the facilitator, Julie the performance system manager and me, Sid, now the planner and past president /CEO. We met in the bank's conference room.

I had prepared information packets, which I now distributed to the group. I began, "I want to thank all of you for your considerable help in creating our liberated workplace and Jim's hands-on help with designing and implementing our system. I'll start by saying that the three most difficult hurdles we overcame were implementing an effective measurement system; getting managers to rely on positive reinforcement; and restructuring the organization from a hierarchical structure to a network structure. These were real challenges and there were several missteps along the way."

Jim exclaimed, "That's surprising. We experienced no problems in our implementation."

There was silence and then everyone laughed loudly at the same time.

I continued, "Well, that said, our results are phenomenal both for the company and personally for our employees. I'll give you a financial overview first. As you know, two years ago Superior Button was on the ropes. Our profits were shrinking due to high costs, poor sales, and customer attrition. Today our costs are down due to reductions in payroll expense and less materials scrap while sales are up due to prospecting for new customers and losing fewer existing accounts. We have also found new raw materials sources and customers in Europe and Asia. I really can't think of anything negative to say."

"Do you expect this success to continue?" Jim asked.

"The biggest change is not financial; it's in the people, including me," I stated. "Conceptually I understood the value of moving from a bureaucratic, subjective, and coercive management system to an objective network system based on positive reinforcement. But seeing the effect on my employees was a true epiphany. They make more money and have more free time. But the real change is deeper than that. It goes to the core of being human. The fundamental change is that they have a direct effect on their environment—on what happens to them. They have control over their work lives that they didn't have before."

I cleared my throat and said, "All the management books that talk about job satisfaction focus on the wrong things. Job satisfaction isn't just about social interactions, pay, benefits, and promotions. More importantly, it's about creating a workplace where people matter, where they see the results of their actions and have the freedom to innovate and expand their capabilities. What we are doing is creating an organization of entrepreneurs—people who take risks in order to secure their own futures.

"Being involved in the transition to a liberated workplace has made me rethink the way I look at our country's social problems. Our public institutions need to make the same transition whether it be education or social programs. As a nation we need to get back to our roots. We need to create schools that are objective, network systems based on positive reinforcement. Teachers and students should have the same workplace we have developed for our employees. We should eliminate the bureaucracies and focus on objective teaching and learning assessment, self-paced learning for students, and a reliance on positive reinforcement to encourage excellent teaching and learning."

Jim chimed in, "The same goes for other governmental programs. I helped the local police department convert their performance system. We measured the crime rate in each policeman's precinct. Starting from a base crime rate, crime-reduction goals were set. They had a large say in how to best reduce the crime rate and different approaches were applied in different precincts. One of the problems with many government programs is that they focus on creating rules and taking coercive action if rules aren't followed. They invariably institute bureaucracies to enforce these rules and as these bureaucracies grow, and they always do, they choke off human initiative and creativity. The one-size-fits-all mentality does not fit with the facts of human diversity in education or the society at large."

Ellen, the bank's facilitator spoke up. "The worst example is the welfare system. You are paid for not working. This system has broken the entrepreneurial spirit of millions of people over the past 50 years or so."

I spoke, "I think a major reason many new educational and social programs fail is that they don't introduce the programs as a gradual transition. Had we not employed a transition strategy at Superior Button, and simply implemented the full program at the start, I'm sure the program would have failed. You need to begin with objective measurement, manager training, and small projects. Then, move to profit-sharing, then stakeholder pay. The measurement system and stakeholder pay set the stage for job enrichment and self-management. To try to move to self-management without these precursors would likely have resulted in failure."

I continued, "One big concern I have is that I am 68-years-old and I am beginning to think about my health and my retirement. To get my investment in the company back, and to fund my retirement, I will need to sell the company. But I'm worried the new owners will tear down the management system we have built and replace it with the more familiar bureaucratic one. Is there anything I can do to prevent this?"

Jim answered, "Have you considered selling the company to your employees? You could start now by implementing an employee stock-option program or ESOP. Stock would only be made available to employees and each employee would decide how much stock they wished to purchase. There are a number of financial benefits in the tax code for you as well. Since they will purchase stock in lieu of performance pay, it's likely that the high performers will invest more and take a larger ownership role. That's just what you would hope for to continue the success of the organization."

"But who will do the planning when I leave?" I asked.

Jim responded, "The employees might hire you as a consultant or you might train a replacement planner, or both. Your risks as a consultant planner vs. an owner would be considerably less and you would be under no obligation to work as a consultant if you became ill or just wanted to do other things."

"That's a great idea and it takes a load off my mind," I said.

I implemented the ESOP the following year, which not only provided for my retirement, but further enhanced Superior Button's employees' commitment to the organization and sense of control over their personal destinies. Now they were complete entrepreneurs in that they were free to choose the best course of action, benefited directly from their efforts, and had an ownership position in the organization.

***

Though technology, markets, and the skills and interests of employees have changed dramatically, the typical workplace has been managed the same way for over a century. An alternative approach to organizational management has been presented that is based on more recent behavioral research and findings. This alternative approach substantially reduces an organization's bureaucracy, replacing it with direct pay to self-managed teams.

The benefits to employees are a reduction in aversive control, increased earnings opportunity and stability, a more flexible work schedule, and more personal control over their work lives. The benefits to the organization are increased productivity and responsiveness and a committed and creative workforce. This book, and my previous ones, describes a practical and proven transition strategy for moving away from the conventional bureaucratic wage-and-salary system toward a self-managed workplace.

ABOUT THE AUTHOR

Dr. Abernathy has consulted in the field of organizational performance systems design and implementation for the past 35 years. He
received his doctorate in industrial/organizational psychology from
Ohio State University. He was a professor at Ohio University before
joining Edward J. Feeney & Associates as a consultant. The firm specialized in applied behavior analysis in business.

He began his own consulting firm, Abernathy & Associates, in
1981. His firm designed performance systems, similar to the one described in this book, for over 170 organizations in banking, insurance,
distribution, health care, transportation, and manufacturing. These organizations ranged in size from small, family-owned businesses to
multinational corporations. They were located across the United States
and in Canada, Guatemala, Mexico, Bermuda, England, France, and
Germany. His company was acquired by Aubrey Daniels International
in 2005. He now teaches industrial/organizational psychology at
Southeastern Louisiana University and has written four books on organizational performance systems.

Books by William Abernathy

Abernathy, W.B. (2012), *Human Performance Diagnostics: A Multidisciplinary Approach to Employee Performance Analysis and Improvement.* Atlanta: Performance Management Publications.

Abernathy, W.B. (2011), *Pay for Profit: Creating an Organization-wide Performance System.* Atlanta: Performance Management Publications.

Abernathy, W.B. (1996), *The Sin of Wages.* Performance Management Press: Atlanta, GA.

www.pManagementPubs.com

ABOUT ADI

Regardless of your industry or expertise, one thing remains constant: People power your business. At Aubrey Daniels International (ADI), we help accelerate the business and safety performance of companies worldwide by using positive, practical approaches grounded in the science of behavior and engineered to ensure long-term sustainability.

Founded in 1978, and headquartered in Atlanta, GA, we work globally with a diverse spectrum of clients. Our clients accelerate strategy execution while fostering employee engagement and positive accountability at all levels of their organization.

ADI provides clients with the tools and methodologies to help move people towards positive, results-driven accomplishments. ADI's products, programs and consulting support help any-one improve their business:

- **Assessments:** scalable, scientific analyses of systems, processes, structures, and practices, and their impact on individual and organizational performance
- **Coaching for Rapid Change®:** a systematic process for focusing managers and leaders to shape positive actions and get change to occur now
- **Surveys:** a complete suite of proprietary surveys to collect actionable feedback on individual and team performance, culture, safety, and other key drivers of business outcomes
- **Certification:** ADI-endorsed mastery of client skills in the training, coaching, and implementation of our key products, processes, and/or technology

Seminars & Webinars: a variety of engaging programs of practical tools and strategies for shaping individual and organizational success

Scorecards & Incentive Pay: an objective and results-focused alternative to traditional incentive pay systems

Safety Solutions: a robust suite of services including surveys, assessments, behavior-based safety, and safety leadership training and coaching, that build an optimal safety culture

Expert Consulting: specialized, hands-on direction and support from seasoned behavioral experts in the design and execution of business-critical strategies and tactics

Speakers: accredited and celebrated thought leaders delivering messages on topics such as sustainability, accelerating performance, and engagement

Blitz Precision Learning®: web-based application for developing, delivering, and administering training lessons that build mastery and fluency

web
aubreydaniels.com
blog
aubreydanielsblog.com
articles
pmezine.com
research
aubreydanielsinstitute.org
social
aubreydaniels.com/follow-us

Performance Management Publications
Additional Resources

 Bringing Out the Best in People

Aubrey C. Daniels

 Measure of a Leader

Aubrey C. Daniels
James E. Daniels

 Other People's Habits

Aubrey C. Daniels

 Safe By Accident

Judy L. Agnew
Aubrey C. Daniels

 Oops!

Aubrey C. Daniels

 Performance Management

Aubrey C. Daniels

 You Can't Apologize to a Dawg!

Tucker Childers

 Removing Obstacles to Safety

Judy L. Agnew
Gail Snyder

 Rapid Change

Joe Laipple

 Pay for Profit

William B. Abernathy

 The Sin of Wages

William B. Abernathy

 Human Performance Diagnostics

William B. Abernathy

For more information call **1.800.223.6191** or visit our Web site
www.PManagementPubs.com

Register Your Book
www.pmanagementpubs.com

Register your copy of
*The Liberated Workplace:
Transitioning to Walden Three*
and receive exclusive reader
benefits. Visit the Web site and
click on the "Register Your
Book" link at the top of the
page. Registration is free.